DESIGNING THE INTERIOR LANDSCAPE

DESIGNING THE INTERIOR LANDSCAPE

RICHARD L. AUSTIN, ASLA

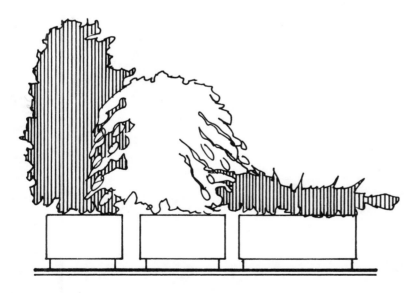

 VAN NOSTRAND REINHOLD COMPANY
————————————————————————————— New York

Printed in the United States of America

Designed by Bernard Stone

Published by Van Nostrand Reinhold Company Inc.
135 West 50th Street
New York, New York 10020

Van Nostrand Reinhold Company Limited
Molly Millars Lane
Wokingham, Berkshire RG11 2PY, England

Van Nostrand Reinhold
480 La Trobe Street
Melbourne, Victoria 3000, Australia

Macmillan of Canada
Division of Canada Publishing Corporation
164 Commander Boulevard
Agincourt, Ontario M1S 3C7, Canada

16 15 14 13 12 11 10 9 8 7 6 5 4 3 2

Library of Congress Cataloging in Publication Data

Austin, Richard L., 1944–
  Designing the interior landscape.

  Bibliography: p.
  Includes index.
  1. Interior landscaping.   2. House plants in interior decoration.   I. Title.
SB419.25.A97   1985   747'.98   84-19674
ISBN 0-442-20930-4
ISBN 0-442-20932-0 (pbk.)

CONTENTS

ACKNOWLEDGMENTS

I wish to take this opportunity to express my appreciation to the following individuals and organizations for their assistance in the preparation of this book: to Mr. Philip R. Cialone, President of Tropical Ornamentals, Inc., Delray Beach, Florida, for assistance in collecting the photographs for the Design Encyclopedia; and to Land Design/Research, Inc., Columbia, Maryland, for the use of planting plan graphics and planting specifications.

PREFACE

The design of the interior landscape is not a random, purposeless activity, a mere decoration of space with plant materials. It is a specific, calculated task that requires the careful consideration of horticultural data and functional alternatives to expand the harmony of our often disorganized lives. Plants add beauty and purpose to our existence, and their placement and use should be cautiously structured for increased personal benefit. Specifically, the design of the interior landscape should:

1. organize and unify interior elements,

2. add identification to an interior space, and

3. expand human reactions to and accommodations of interior surroundings.

In organizing and unifying interior elements, plant materials separate potentially conflicting spaces by providing physical barriers between uses. Through attractive site lines and directional components, plants bring visually separated spaces together, allowing them to function as one space. Plants often identify an area as a "people space" when hanging baskets and colorful annuals are added. Solar porches and spacious patios would be less desirable if plants were not present.

One of the most interesting advantages plants offer is the expansion of our tolerance to our environments. Just as light, temperature, and water allow individual plants to adapt to their environment, plant materials allow us to adapt to the designed interior. Our homes, offices, and shopping centers simply become more livable when plants are present.

Essentially, the interior landscape will function as a supportive feature to a people-oriented space. Although some compositions are structured for commercial purposes, such as vegetable gardens or cut-flower operations, most are decorative in function and require great attention to detail.

To implement an interior landscape, a designer should base the organization of the materials upon the principles of landscape architecture, interior design, and horticultural science. (fig. P-1).

For landscape architecture, it is important to consider the elements of color, form, texture, scale, balance, and the accent of plant materials. For interior design, it is important to consider the organization for decoration, the accommodation of people to a physical space, and safety factors. For horticultural science, it is important to consider the specific soil, moisture, light, and maintenance requirements for the supportive habitat.

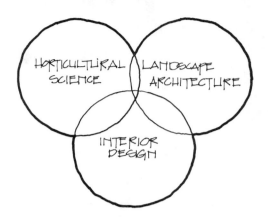

P-1. The design of the interior landscape combines the issues of horticulture and the design applications of both landscape architecture and interior design.

1/DESIGN

The Design Elements

It is best to approach the arrangement of the interior landscape in much the same way as one would approach an exterior composition: with careful intent and specific implementation. The design intent, or objectives of the project, must be clearly understood and stated by both client and designer. Without an organized approach to the solution, the end result may be a disorganized concoction of ill-suited vegetation.

The selection of the plant material for an interior composition should be based upon the specific functions they are to serve within the space. Are they to create a specific shape, emphasize a specific area, or support specific architectural elements? If the uses of the plant materials are not considered, the resource commitments for the project may be wasted.

The first element to consider in plant selection should be *physical characteristics*: the color, form, or texture qualities it may have. The second is *perceptual characteristics*: the qualities for supporting accent, scale, sequence, and balance. These physical and perceptual characteristics are the basic tools a designer will use to create the environment.

The Physical Characteristics

COLOR

Color is dependent upon the wavelength of the light reflected from an object. Because of this, it is the most striking of all the design elements, both in landscape and interior design, and will attract attention to a specific part of the composition more quickly than any other element will. It can influence emotions, create specific feelings, and add beauty and harmony to a designed environment.

The psychological effects of color are generally the same for most people, although color preference and impact vary among individuals. For example, reds, yellows, and oranges are warm and active colors and tend to unite design compositions because of their apparent brightness. When objects within the space have these colors, they seem to be larger than they really are; thus the illusion of *advancement* is created. Blues, greens, or violets are cooler in their effect and plants or objects of these colors will appear smaller than they actually are. This is the illusion of *receding* color.

There are two types of color that must be considered by the designer in an interior planting composition. The first is background or *basic* color; this includes the colors of the walls, ceilings, and floors. These hues should guide the selections of the foliage and flowering characteristics of plant material. The second type is the *accent* color, which is the actual physical appearance of the plants. This type is often difficult to achieve with the more common foliage materials. To portray a bright appearance, some plants need more light than is available in low-light interiors. It may be necessary to supplement the design with colorful planters, sculptures,

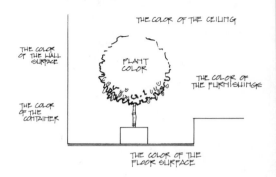

1-1. The color of the plant should work with the colors of its surroundings.

or other architectural features to achieve eye-attracting accents.

The following general principles should be considered when using color in an interior composition:

1. People have a psychological tendency to move in the direction of light or vivid colors. Colors can therefore be used to direct people within the space to specific, functional areas.

2. Some plants will not bloom or show bright, attractive foliage characteristics if there is no high source of light. Thus, artificial light sources may be required.

3. The applications of color and how they will appear to the person within the interior space are influenced by the distance at which they are viewed, the amount of direct or indirect light, the amount of shade, and the soil conditions within the planting container.

FORM

Every plant or group of plants in the interior landscape has a distinct natural form that will establish specific functional characteristics. Although most specimen plants are artificially sculptured for specific visual effects, the most common shapes are round, oval, upright, weeping or drooping, and spreading or horizontal (fig. 1-2). These different forms are used individually and in group massings to support the architectural features within the composition space.

As individual characteristics, the various shapes of plants bring specific features to a design. Vertical forms, for instance, help create strong accents and add visual height to a space (fig. 1-3). Horizontal forms add width and direct the eye to specific areas along the floors (fig. 1-4). Weeping or drooping forms create soft connecting lines between objects and often tie vertical forms and horizontal forms together (fig. 1-5). These are important considerations when the designer must move pedestrians in the direction of their "eye-flow."

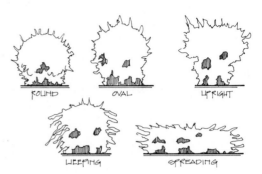

1-2. Common shapes of plants.

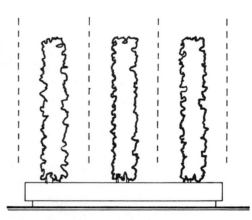

1-3. Vertical forms tend to direct the eye up and down, creating strong accents.

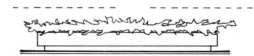

1-4. Horizontal forms tend to direct the eye to each side for a supporting accent.

Rounded or globular forms are useful in creating large plant masses for enclosures (fig. 1-6). It is best to use these forms as the element of unification throughout the composition and then support the design with the other forms as accent features.

Individual plant forms can be combined to create different planting arrangements for different interior effects (fig. 1-7). When this is done, the combination of the plants in the arrangement should take precedence over that of the individual plant. This application of forms is desirable when uniquely shaped plants are not available. By combining the various forms to create a special effect, the designer will have a greater range of plant applicability.

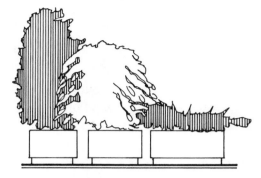

1-5. Weeping or drooping forms often tie vertical and horizontal forms together.

TEXTURE

Texture, one of the most important of the design elements, is the visual or tactile surface quality of any plant. It should be considered in relation to the plants, the containers, and the surroundings in which they are placed (fig. 1-8).

Texture may also be qualified in terms of the distance from which the plants are viewed. The perceived size of the units varies with changes in distance. When we are close enough to touch a plant, we are able to see the quality of the individual leaves and the texture of the leaf surfaces. At a distance, we see the leaves only in the aggregate, not as individual units. Texture then becomes the entire mass.

In the interior landscape, texture is the arrangement and size of the leaves, stems, branches, or containers and is described by qualities of coarseness or fineness, roughness or smoothness, heaviness or lightness, thickness or thinness. In applying texture to a design composition, the designer must make sure that each part of the plant is related in such a way that it functions with the materials surrounding it. If the textures change, they must do so in a logical and graduated manner. They should generally proceed in a *sequence* and not break continuity (fig. 1-9).

1-6. Rounded forms are best used as enclosing elements. Other forms may then be used for accent.

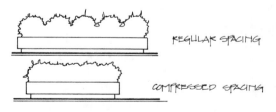

1-7. Regular spacing will show off individual forms whereas compressed spacing will unite the plant materials into a more dominant form.

Texture also has certain psychological and physical effects upon people. For example, as textures change in sequence, they can make the space seem smaller or larger than it actually is: a coarse-to-fine sequence can make a space seem larger, while a sequence of fine to coarse may make it seem smaller. Coarse-textured, large-leafed plants should not be used in small spaces if they are meant to be inconspicuous. Fine-textured, small-leafed plants should not be used in large spaces if they are meant to be dominant features in a design (fig. 1-10).

The Perceptual Characteristics

ACCENT

An accent is a visual break in a sequence or pattern of plant material. It has a dramatic effect on the visual appearance of an interior environment by concentrating attention on a specific portion of the design and playing upon the natural perceptions of the viewer. Since one usually views an interior landscape while walking through the space, with attention varying from minute to minute, the use of the accent element in an interior space can capture the attention of the viewer and control how the composition is both seen and used.

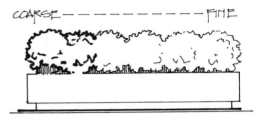

1-9. The texture sequence should move from *fine* to *coarse* or vice versa. This will expand the continuity of the composition.

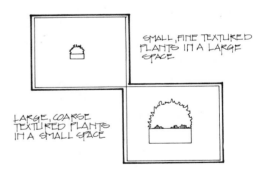

1-10. For textural accents to be more effective in the composition, do not use small, fine-textured plants within a large interior or large, coarse-textured plants within a small interior.

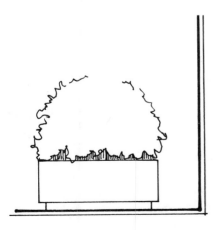

1-8. As with color, the texture of a plant must be compared with its surroundings before it can function properly within the composition.

For an accent to be effective, it must be strong. The human eye, with its ability to see peripherally, tends to wander aimlessly. It is important to remember that too many accents within the "visual cone" will confuse the viewer and reduce the effect of the feature. The use of strong accents (fig. 1-11) demands and captures attention.

Accents may be created with the use of colors, forms, and textures. If the dominant pattern in a space tends to be a fine texture, a plant with a medium or coarse texture will stand out as the accent feature (the one with coarse texture more strongly than the one with medium texture). An abrupt change in form or color from the more dominant element will create a strong accent.

A contrast in the spacing of plants within the design composition will serve as a point of accent. Plant materials placed in a sequential order never attract attention until one of the units disappears. This gap is eye-catching and will serve as a good interior accent (fig. 1-12).

BALANCE

Balance is the state of equipoise between design elements. It is the visual sense a designer has of how plant masses, colors, textures, and forms are used and how they appear to the viewer. In an interior composition, two types of balance are considered: *formal* or symmetrical, which is the repetition of features on both sides of the central axis; and *informal* or asymmetrical, the variation of plant type, quality, or position on either side of the central axis (fig. 1-13).

The Architectural Forms of Plants

Because a plant occupies space, it appears as a specific architectural design form. For the interior landscape, these forms may be defined as follows:

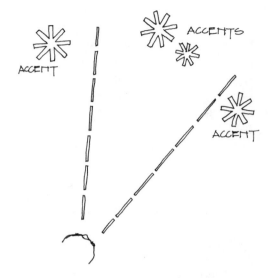

1-11. Too many accent features within the visual cone create confusion within the composition.

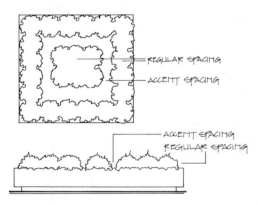

1-12. A visual break in the spacing of similar plants will help create stronger accents.

1. The *screen* is a plant or plant mass used as a total enclosure of a space. A person within the space cannot walk or see through this form (fig. 1-14). A screen may be created with a single plant, a plant mass, or a combination of plants with other architectural elements.

2. The *canopy* is a plant or plant mass with a branching height of 7′ (2.1 m) or more, which will allow an individual to walk underneath (fig. 1-15). Its most important design characteristic is that it occupies only the overhead plane.

3. The *barrier* is a plant or plant mass used as a partial enclosure or as a control of circulation within an interior space. A person may see over this feature but not walk through it (fig. 1-16).

4. The *baffle* is a plant or plant mass used to control visual experiences wthin the interior landscape. An individual may see through but cannot walk through it (fig. 1-17). A baffle may be created by a plant or plant mass that does not interrupt the visual experience but that does act as a physical barrier.

5. The *groundcover* is a plant or plant mass used as a visual floor, usually reaching a maximum height of 18″ (45.7 cm). Groundcover may be created, however, by keeping it below the eye level of the viewer (fig. 1-18).

These architectural forms may be used to create numerous and varied interior compositions, but their effectiveness as design features depend upon the following:

1. type, age, and condition of the plant materials,

2. spacing of the plants, which determines the opacity, translucency, or transparency of the element, and

3. form and growth rate of the individual plants, which affect the density of the total element. (Density is affected by the shape and size of the leaves, branching patterns, branching heights, and the height and width of the plant when planted and when mature.)

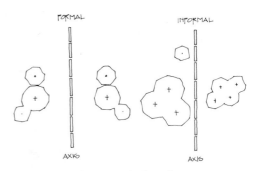

1-13. Symmetrical and asymmetrical balance.

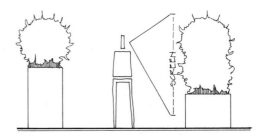

1-14. For a plant to function as a screen, it must block the visual spectrum.

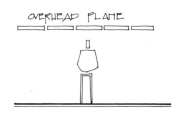

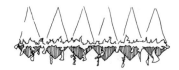

A- THE CANOPY MUST OCCUPY THE OVERHEAD PLANE TO FUNCTION PROPERLY.

1-16. The barrier must interrupt pedestrian circulation to function properly.

B -A MASS OF HANGING BASKETS CAN BE USED AS AN EFFECTIVE CANOPY.

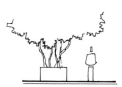

C- THE MOST COMMON CANOPY IS A LARGE TREE THAT OCCUPIES THE OVERHEAD PLANE.

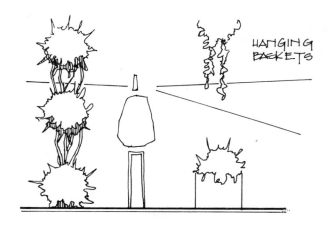

1-17. The baffle must prevent movement through the space while allowing visual experiences to occur.

1-15. (A) The canopy must occupy the overhead plane to function properly.
(B) A mass of hanging baskets can be used as an effective canopy.
(C) The most common canopy is a large tree that occupies the overhead plane.

The Interior Design Components

As a designer considers the effects of a single plant or plant mass on the interior environment, additional thought must be given to the way in which the viewer will react within the composition. The elements of color, form, texture, accent, and balance are the basic considerations in the application of various design components to a finished space. Combined with the architectural forms, the design components magnify the character of the molded space and allow the designer to control the way in which the space is both seen and felt by the viewer.

The *primary interior design components* are the physical units that support the design:

1. *Direction* moderates the physical movement within a space. A designer may control the visual experiences within the composition by allowing movement only in a specific direction or area (fig. 1-19).

2. *Pooling,* on the other hand, defines the "rooms" desired by the designer (fig. 1-20). Because viewers are directed throughout a composition, it may be desirable to expand the size of the perceived space and alter the experiences.

The *secondary interior design components* are the visual/psychological units that support the composition:

1. *Enframement* draws attention to a focal area or important view within the space. It may be accomplished by using plants that project into the visual plane and outline a specific feature within the composition.

2. *Linkage* visually joins one space or object to another space or object (fig. 1-21).

3. *Enlargement* or *reduction* is the ability to change the apparent size of the composition. It may be accomplished by varying the degree of enclosure of the space.

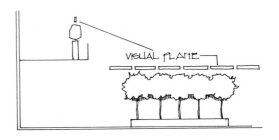

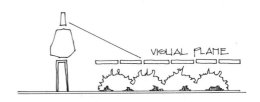

1-18. A groundcover must be lower than eye level to be effective.

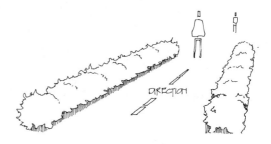

1-19. Plants assist in supporting pedestrian movement by defining direction.

4. *Invitation* uses stimulation, suggestion, or curiosity to pull a viewer into or through space. It may be accomplished with moving objects or with bright, sudden changes of color.

5. *Subdivision* is the use of interior plant materials to divide a large space into smaller components or to create a small space within a large one.

A Process for Design

In order to facilitate an orderly and successful attainment of objectives in an interior planting composition, it is important to follow a development process that will solve intricate spatial problems. This assumes, however, that the purpose of the interior landscape is more than decoration. If a client or designer merely wants to add material for cosmetic adornment, then a process may be a waste of valuable time for the installer. On the other hand, a process can be used to illustrate that plant materials have a specific function to perform, and their inclusion in the space adds a unique and valuable dimension to the final investment.

The following development process is only one of several that can be adopted to complete an interior planting composition. It is not a universal solution, but one that can expand the understanding of *how* and *why* plants are used in the space. For clients who do not always understand the benefits of vegetation, it should expand their awareness. For clients who do understand, it should support their efforts for a pleasing and unique environment.

Phase One: Preplanning Considerations

The initial phase of any process should include the gathering of information pertinent to the design and the planting of the environment. The quality and extent of the information collected during this phase has a direct influence over sub-

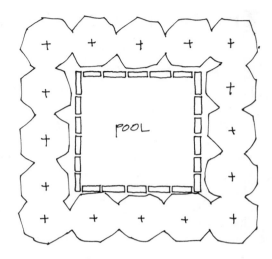

1-20. When plants define an "indoor" room, the effect of *pooling* is created.

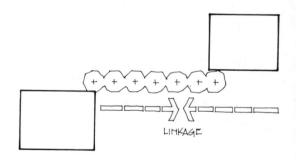

1-21. When plants visually join two spaces together, the effect of *linkage* is created.

sequent analysis and decision-making steps. Care must be taken to collect information that is current and specifically related to the proposed environment.

STEP ONE: DEVELOP DESIGN OBJECTIVES
The client or client group has very specific objectives in mind when a development is contemplated. He, she, or they may want to make a shopping center more "gardenlike" to encourage visitation—which in turn encourages more impulse buying by consumers. Reducing the psychological sterility of an office or home is very often a specific objective of many clients who wish to stress "people interactions." Whatever the goals, the designer must first identify these issues and relate them in terms of design objectives or design intent.

STEP TWO: DETERMINE SPACE CAPACITIES
The most honorable of goals may terminate abruptly if the space considered for development cannot support the desired objectives. This research step examines the capability of the space to satisfy the *design intent*. The principal area of research involves physical information: habitat conditions and circulation within the space. *Habitat* will determine the placement of plant material in relation to the proper growing environment, while *circulation* will determine the placement in relation to the support of or interference with people.

Of the three most important habitat elements—light, water, and soil—light is the critical factor of this step. Water and soils can be more easily controlled within the containers. Light, however, requires a more extensive analysis before the final placement is made.

Within this step, therefore, a *light-intensity map* can be developed; this will illustrate the zones of usable light within the space (fig. 1-22). From this map, directions can be given for the construction or placement of plant containers. If built-in containers exist, it will determine what plants may be the most suitable for the location.

In addition to the light-intensity map, a *circulation map*

can be developed to aid in determining the most appropriate locations for accent materials, barriers, baffles, or even pools (fig. 1-23). It will also indicate the potential locations for maintenance problems caused by "people blight."

STEP THREE: DETERMINE DEVELOPMENT LIMITATIONS

Given the design intent and the results of the space capacity research, the designer should be able to set forth specific development limitations and suggest alternatives that would satisfy the goals and objectives of the project. Three alternatives can be envisioned at this step: all the client objectives can be satisfied by the space; a portion of the objectives can be met, with minor alterations in either the client program or the space features; or none of the objectives can be met without major and costly modifications of the program or spatial features. It is at this step of the process that the designer and/or client should determine whether the project should be continued or abandoned (fig. 1-24).

1-22. For large spaces, the light-intensity map can be developed by using a light meter to determine the low, medium, and high light areas of the space. Several readings should be made at different times of the day for an average evaluation.

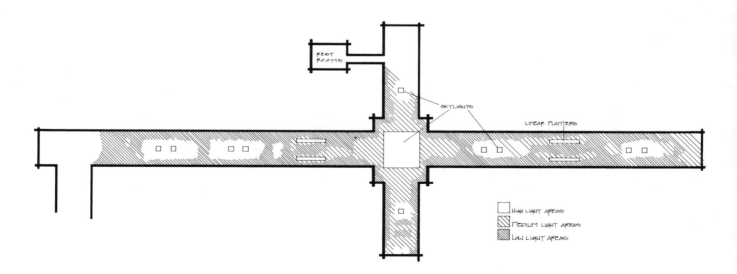

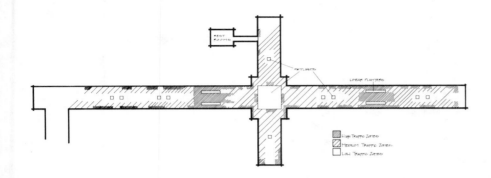

1-23. By observing the usage of the site or by making predictions from architectural drawings, the circulation map can determine where plants might be placed to avoid problem areas.

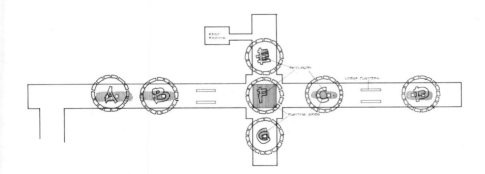

1-24. By evaluating the design intent and the results of the space capacity research, the designer should be able to determine specific development limitations and suggest alternatives that would satisfy the goals and objectives of the project.

Phase Two: Developing the Plan

This phase consists of the arrangement of basic design elements into a preliminary set of design concepts that will fulfill the intended client program. With continued input from the client, the designer begins to formulate specific decision-making steps necessary for the development of the final plan.

STEP ONE: DEVELOP THE PLANTING CONCEPTS

This step involves the use of plant material to reinforce the architectural character of the space. By using the physical characteristics of plants (color, form, and texture), the designer can select a specific accent, scale sequence, or balance the space is to have. From this, the architectural forms can be employed to create vistas or resting areas for the visitors to enjoy. Direction or pooling components can be enhanced, or the division of spaces can result. These issues, when represented graphically, are the planting concepts proposed for the space (fig. 1-25).

1-25.

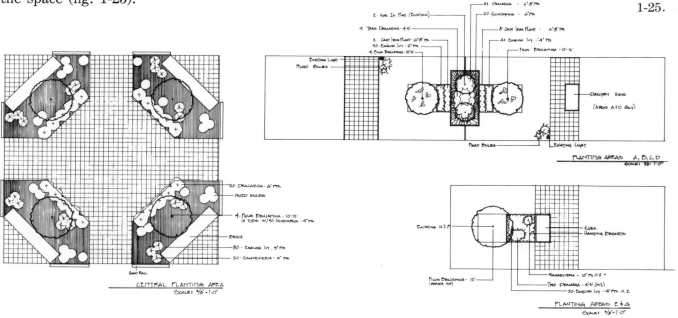

STEP TWO: PREPARE THE FINAL PLAN

If all the alternatives have been discussed and considered and the planting concepts meet the intended objectives, the final planting plan should be completed. Client input should be continually maintained, even though this is the final step of the design phase.

Phase Three: Implementation

This final phase provides the client assistance in seeing that the design product actually comes to life. Support and implementation information provide the vital link in the chain of design communication.

STEP ONE: DOCUMENTS PREPARATION

Develop the planting and construction details, installation and planting specifications, and maintenance requirements of the plan. The elements of the design may need to be communicated to a possible third party for approval. Make sure that all the necessary data have been presented.

STEP TWO: INSTALLATION

Although the basic design phases have been completed, installation may require changes to comply with unforeseen problems. A periodic review of the procedures selected and employed to achieve the design should be maintained.

STEP THREE: EVALUATION

The plant material selected may be growing and prospering in its new home, but the designer's function has not ended. As plants grow and mature, so does their relationship to their environment. These changes should be evaluated in order to learn from mistakes of selection and judgment.

2/HABITATS

While composing the exterior landscape, a designer takes into account the factors of light, temperature, moisture, and soil conditions when determining the adaptability of the plant material. The movement of the sun, shade patterns, and reflected light are important ingredients for the effective placement of flowering vegetation. Exposure to varying temperatures alters the ability of the plant to perform its design function. Water must be available to assist in the life-support systems for the plants, and soils provide the nutrients for uniform growth.

With few exceptions, the design considerations for the exterior environment are the same as those for the interior environment. The major differences occur in the controllability of interior growing conditions compared to exterior. In interior environments, when a light source is insufficient for plant growth, more light can be added; damaging temperatures can be changed and held relatively constant if necessary;

moisture can be placed into or removed from the air; and poor soils can be replaced or improved without a great deal of effort. In an exterior garden, these changes would be enormously expensive.

It is important to remember that the habitat should be designed to maintain a relatively constant growth rate for the plant materials. An overdesigned habitat may cause the plants to grow excessively. This creates a changing design and expensive plant-maintenance programs. An underdesigned habitat, on the other hand, causes plants to wither and die, which necessitates continuous replacement. The properly designed habitat, therefore, is one that stabilizes plant growth to the extent that leaves that drop off are replaced. The color, form, texture, or size of the artistic element changes very little.

Lighting

The most important of the four habitat elements is light. A plant must have light to convert the elements it obtains from food sources into energy that sustains growth. Often, a plant can survive in insufficient light for extended periods and still look attractive. Before long, however, the stored food reserves will be depleted and the plant soon becomes weak and unattractive. A recovery period will then be necessary before it can perform its intended design function.

The actual amount of light a plant needs is more than most designers realize. Measured light inside a building is drastically different from the outside. Shaded windows and skylights allow only a small portion of the sun's rays to penetrate an area for plant usage. Outside, in the summer, a plant could receive as much as 15,000 footcandles, while next to an exposed skylight or window, it could receive as little as 50 footcandles. Both extremes could easily cause the plant to wither and die.

In order to adequately evaluate a space for interior landscaping, it is important to check each possible planting location with a light meter (fig. 2-1). This instrument will identify the areas of both sufficient and insufficient light for the support of the plants. There are several techniques for recording these data, but the most efficient is the grid method (fig. 2-2). This allows the designer to plot graphically the locations where plants will receive the most effective light for growth and development. There are, however, zones of insufficient light, such as those that may exist between two skylights, where plants will have a difficult time adapting. For instance, although a meter reading may indicate acceptable conditions, some plants tend to bend toward a more powerful light source if improperly placed in these zones (fig. 2-3).

Because of the current trend toward more energy-efficient buildings and homes, the sources of light are beginning to dwindle. Tinted glass and reduced lighting fixtures are now commonplace, and the "natural" sources through ceiling skylights may be less adequate than before. The designer should consider supplementing an area with artificial light if an extensive landscape is contemplated. The most available sources for this light are the incandescent and fluorescent lamps found in most interior areas.

Incandescent lamps differ widely in shape and efficiency (fig. 2-4). No special equipment is needed to use them in a design, and they are available as spot or flood lamps in various wattage intensities. Their advantages include:

1. compact light source,
2. low installation costs,
3. wide range of available sizes, and
4. high level of red light.

Some disadvantages, however also exist:

1. low energy efficiency,
2. excessive heat,
3. short life,

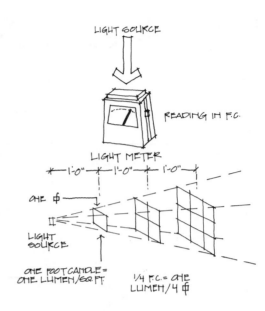

2-1. A light meter will help identify the areas of sufficient and insufficient lighting. One footcandle (fc) is equal to one lumen one square foot from the source.

4. frequent nonuniform distribution of light,

5. intensity not always sufficient for flowering plants, and

6. low level of blue light.

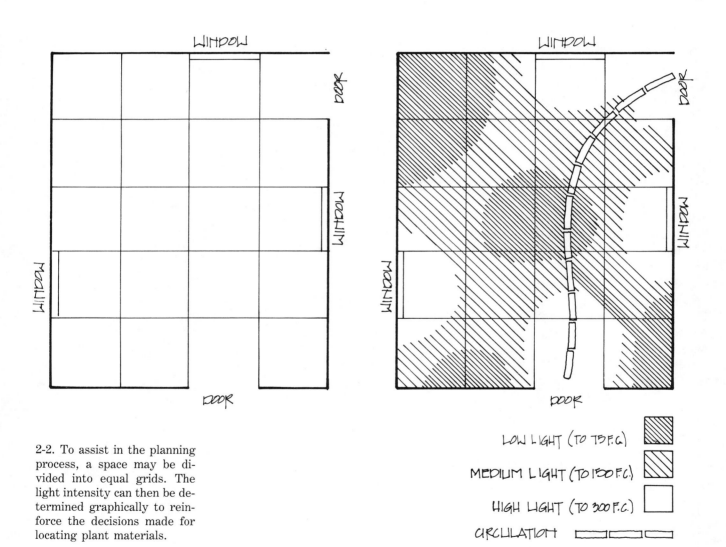

2-2. To assist in the planning process, a space may be divided into equal grids. The light intensity can then be determined graphically to reinforce the decisions made for locating plant materials.

LOW LIGHT (TO 75 F.C.)

MEDIUM LIGHT (TO 150 F.C.)

HIGH LIGHT (TO 300 F.C.)

CIRCULATION

Fluorescent lamps are usually the best source for artificial light. The low-pressure mercury lamp types offer better-quality light for growth and maintenance in the environment. The specific advantages to these units are:

1. more energy efficiency,
2. less heat production than in incandescent lamps,
3. longer life than incandescent lamps,
4. much better light distribution, and
5. high level of blue light.

Disadvantages for their use include:

1. more expensive installation than incandescent,
2. light intensity cannot be focused,
3. lower tube efficiency on each end than in the middle (fig. 2-5), and
4. low level of red light.

The quality of light a plant receives is another important issue. When visible light passes through a prism, the colors range from violet to red. These colors play an important part in the selection of plants for a design composition. As the length of time a plant is exposed to a light source changes, so do the growth habits of the plants. Too much *red light*, for instance, may promote stem elongation in some plants. A low *blue light* may cause phototropism (the bending of the plant toward a light source). Essentially, plants need a balance of red and blue light for maximum efficiency.

Temperature

The second most important habitat element is temperature. Plant growth and survival depend upon an adequate range of temperature. For most interior foliage materials, a range of 65° to 75°F (18° to 24°C) is considered sufficient.

The most damaging factor is temperature fluctuation.

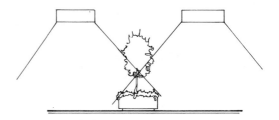

2-3. The upper portions of a larger plant may have a tendency to bend toward a powerful light source.

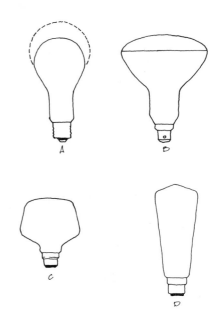

2-4. The most popular types of incandescent lamps used in the interior landscape include standard (*A*), flood (*B*), and decorative (*C* and *D*).

Thermostats are usually lowered at night for increased energy efficiency. In a residential composition, the damage may be less severe than in a commercial space where the temperature may remain lowered over the weekend or holiday period. If the fluctuation becomes excessive, physical injury to the plant system will occur.

Too much hot air will be harmful to most plants because this causes an excessive loss of water, which results in wilting and a breakdown of the plant tissues. If heat must be added to an interior environment, it should be done gradually so the possible damage can be minimized. Too much cold air directed at the plant will injure its vital systems and create wilting, injury, and eventual death (fig. 2-6).

Moisture

Water is the raw material that affects the growth and development of the plant cells. An adequate supply of this element must be made available to the plant at all times. However, providing too much water is usually the most serious mistake the designer can make: excess water prevents oxygen from reaching the plant and often kills the root system.

Applying water to a composition can be as complicated or simple as the design allows. For large planting areas, a built-in water source may be best. For small locations, a water-holding container can be provided. The actual system for delivering the water will vary from design to design (fig. 2-7).

The optimum humidity for most areas can be created mechanically if necessary. Commercial humidifiers readily provide a source for this moisture. A range of 30 to 60 percent relative humidity satisfies the majority of foliage plants. For some exotic displays, however, more sophisticated techniques may be needed (fig. 2-8).

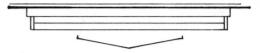

2-5. The middle portion of the fluorescent tube is the most efficient.

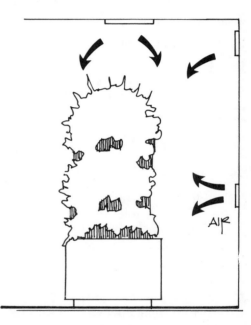

2-6. Exposure to air movement from vents within the space can alter the available moisture and temperature requirements for the plants.

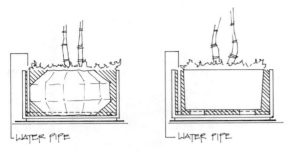

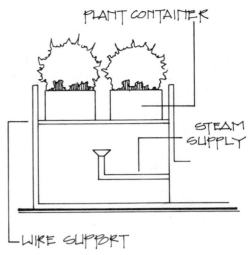

2-7. The plant on the left has been planted directly into the decorative planter, with a water pipe installed along the side. On the right, the plant has been placed into the decorative planter, with the waterpipe supplying moisture through the bottom of the container.

2-8. When a more exotic plant species is used and a steam supply is required, the moisture should be allowed to reach the plants from below.

Soil

The type of soils used for the interior composition depends largely upon the type of plants being used in the design. Basically, soils that will hold moisture and yet allow the drainage of excess water should be chosen. Waterlogged soil is a prime factor in the death of indoor plants.

Physical condition and functional texture are often more important than the chemical composition of a soil because fertilizers can be added to a well-structured soil to stimulate plant growth.

Common sandy loam soil is rarely capable of supporting plants in an interior landscape. Additives must be included in the planting mixture if optimum growing conditions are to be achieved. The ideal medium is one that contains 50 percent solid material and 50 percent pore space (25 percent water and 25 percent air).

2-9. Sphagnum moss is an excellent planting material as well as a mulch for containers.

The more common materials that can be added to a sandy loam soil include the following:

1. *Sphagnum peat moss* (the horticultural grade is recommended) assists in the retention of moisture and is acid in reaction (fig. 2-9).

2. *Wood chips* can be used for a soil mix (very small particles) or mulch (larger chips)

3. *Sand,* used more to increase drainage and aeration, should be sterilized before it is placed into the mix (fig. 2-10).

4. *Vermiculite,* a sterile mica compound, is easily compressed and is not as durable as sand or perlite. It will increase the water-holding capacity of the soil (fig. 2-11).

5. *Perlite,* a volcanic material, is easy to use and is sterile. It improves drainage and aeration in the mix (fig. 2-12).

Most interior plants, except cacti, prefer a more organic soil base. The following mixtures are the most common:

Basic Potting Soil
- 1 part garden loam
- 1 part coarse sand or perlite
- 1 part peat moss

Acid-loving Mixture
- 1 part garden loam
- 2 parts peat moss
- 1 part sand or perlite

Cacti and Succulent Soil Mixture
- 1 part garden loam
- 3 parts sand
- 1 part peat moss

2-10. Sterilized sand is good for increasing the drainage capability of soil mixes.

2-11. Vermiculite is good for increasing the water-holding capacity of the planting mix.

2-12. Aeration and drainage can be improved with the use of perlite.

3/INSTALLATION

The actual selection of the location for plant material in the interior landscape is one of the most important issues a designer will face. Improperly placed materials create excessive installation costs, steadily increasing maintenance costs, and the rapid deterioration of plants. Any one of these factors can easily deter a client from developing an interior landscape. Therefore, a review of their special significance to the design of an environment is critical.

Plant Containers

When designing interior spaces, the architectural feature that will contain the plant will directly influence the installation costs for the project. Far too often, plants are selected to fit the planters, which is very poor design judgment. The planter should instead be designed or selected to fit the plant needed for the space (fig. 3-1).

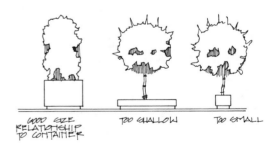

3-1. The container should be selected to fit the plant first, and then the space. An incorrect container will shorten the design effectiveness of the material.

Assuming the habitat conditions are already acceptable, the actual container that supports the plant will determine the success or failure of the design. It can be either a stationary (built-in) or a movable type—whichever is best for the plant material. Specifically, it must meet the physical needs of the material; it must have adequate space for root growth and development; it must have proper drainage to prevent the buildup of salts; it must be durable enough to withstand the weight of soil and moisture pushing against its sides; it must function within the constraints of the design; and it must be attractive (fig. 3-2).

The specific materials used for the construction of the planter are as variable as the designs. The following are some of the many different types of available materials:

Decorative metals are often used as a sleeve cover around the more standard plant container. Because of the toxic agents often used to process these units, it may be best not to place the root systems directly in touch with the container.

Concrete and stone can often provide a natural effect for the interior environment. Different casting forms can add interesting variations for increased textural appeal. Concrete is often cast-in-place, but some commercial types are movable. Natural stone is an excellent choice for permanent planters with a dry-stone or mortared construction.

Ceramic can be applied to a composition in an infinite number of ways. It is often heavy, however, and is easily broken if moved too much.

Fiberglass containers are nonporous, lightweight, and available in almost any color or color combination. Some, however, are not colorfast and may eventually fade. Extremely cold temperatures may also cause them to shatter.

Wood is a common material used for planters and planter sleeves. In most instances, it is durable, attractive, and meets the specifications of both plant and design. Some woods, however, may have been treated with preservatives that are toxic to the plant materials. To extend the life of the planter and to prevent staining from moisture, a plastic or metal

3-2. These stationary planters in the Hyatt Regency in Chicago, Illinois, are incorporated into the fountain design for a more creative effect. (Courtesy of Land Design/Research, Inc.)

insert should be used with most wooden planters.

Although the material of the plant container is important to the overall composition, the successful interior landscape incorporates the containers into the architectural character of the space as well. In the past, portable planters were added more as an afterthought for decorative effect. Today, however, the creative designer merges the foliage into the space with such care and consideration that the plants seem to belong to the space. Movable units should be used to support permanent ones for such functions as cut-flower or specimen rotation programs.

If the intent of the design programs is to be achieved, the planting areas and the specific containers should be selected with great care. One unique but seldom-used arrangement is the suspended planter. Although the hanging systems are very heavy (usually over 50 to 60 pounds per cubic foot of soil, plus the weight of the plant), they can be extremely useful for creating special effects. If a specimen rotation program is part of the design, hanging baskets of colorful annuals or foliage materials can be used to splash accents throughout an environment. Some creative applications of planters are shown in figures 3-3 through 3-9.

3-3. The planters should be a part of the overall design rather than an addition to it. (Courtesy of Land Design/ Research, Inc.)

3-4. The design function of these materials is enhanced through the design of the planting space. (Courtesy of Land Design/Research, Inc.)

3-5. Without the addition of interior plant material, this designed space would be less inviting. (Courtesy of Land Design/Research, Inc.)

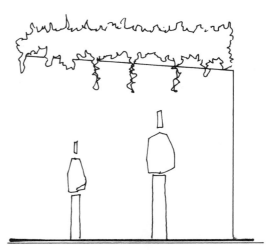

3-6. Overhead beams can be hidden by the creative application of hanging planters.

3-7. Plants can be built into walls, backlighted, and used to display unique specimen materials. Glass fronts will allow children to view the developing root systems.

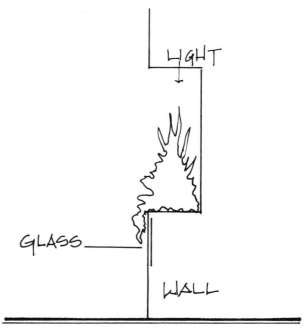

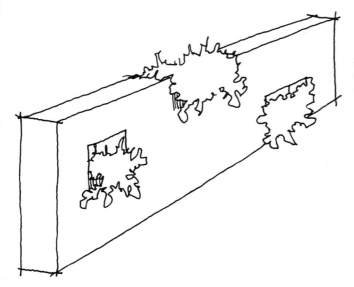

3-8. Wall masses can be softened with the application of creative planters.

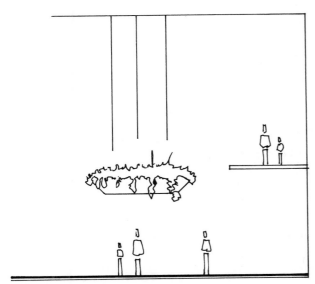

3-9. Large hanging plants can function as both overhead canopies and groundcovers.

Installation Specifications

If a designer is not directly involved in the installation of the plant materials, it is best to provide an accurate set of installation specifications. This information for bidders will determine the final appearance of the environment and, therefore, this communication link to the contractor is important. The following is a general guide to the preparation of this document (adapted from specifications furnished by Land Design/Research, Inc.).

1. *Conditions of Work*

Each bidder must be fully informed of the conditions relating to the construction of the project and the employment of labor thereon. Failure to do so will not relieve a successful bidder of the obligation to furnish all material and labor necessary to carry out the provisions of the contract. Insofar as possible, the contractor, in carrying out the work, must employ such methods or means as will not cause any interruption of, or interference with, the work of any other contractor.

2. *Addenda and Interpretations*

No interpretation of the meaning of the plans, specifications, or other prebid documents will be made orally to any bidder. Every request for such interpretation should be in writing addressed to the designer and, to be given consideration, must be received at least five days prior to the date fixed for the opening of bids. Any and all such interpretations and any supplemental instructions will be in the form of written addenda to the specifications which, if issued, will be mailed by certified mail with return receipt requested to all prospective bidders (at the respective addresses furnished for such purposes), no later than three days prior to the date fixed for the opening of bids. Failure of any bidder to receive any such addendum or interpretation shall not relieve such bidder from any obligation under the bid as submitted. All addenda so issued shall become part of the contract documents.

3. *Tree Placement and Location*
It is understood that each bidder will establish the location of all specified plant material before submitting a bid.

4. *Tagging and Approval of Plant Material*
All trees must be tagged by the contractor in the nursery. The contractor must then submit a request for approval of tagged trees to the landscape architect. Approval must be given before trees will be accepted for planting.

5. *Definitions*

01 SCOPE:
Furnish all material, labor, and equipment necessary to completely install all interior planting as shown on the drawings and specified herein.

02 MATERIALS:
Planting Mixture: The material to be used in all planters and plant tubs shall be a soilless landscape mix such as Metro-Mix 200. This material is a premixed blend of sphagnum peat moss, vermiculite, perlite, and other horticultural ingredients as manufactured by (company name).

In planters where the depth of growing medium will exceed 12″ (30.4 cm), placement of growing medium shall be in layers 6″ to 12″ (15.2 to 30.4 cm) thick. Each layer shall be thoroughly "wet-out" and worked with rakes before the next layer is installed.

If a substitute plant mixture is used, a certified analysis of its ingredients and its blending procedures shall be submitted to the landscape architect for approval before delivery to the site. If deficiencies in the mixture are found as a result of this analysis, they shall be corrected at no expense to the owner.

03 PLANT MATERIALS:
A. Quality and Size: Plant material shall conform to

the sizes given in the plant list, shall be sound, healthy, vigorous, and free from plant diseases and insect pests or their eggs, and shall have normal, healthy root systems. All measurements such as spread, ball, or container size, number of stems, and quality designations shall be in accordance with the latest standards of the American Association of Nurserymen. Shrubs planted in rows or massing shall be uniform in shape and size.

B. Substitutions: These will be permitted only upon submission of proof that specified plants are not obtainable and with the authorization of the landscape architect to provide for the use of the nearest equivalent, size, and variety of plants. All requests for price adjustments due to substitutions will be submitted in writing to the landscape architect and owner's representative for approval along with a request for use of the substitution.

C. Inspection: All major plant material such as trees shall be approved at the source by the landscape architect or representative before delivery to the site. The landscape architect reserves the right to reject any plant material that does not meet the quality standards as specified.

D. Protection During and After Delivery: Due to the tenderness of the foliage of tropical plant material, the following specifications must be strictly adhered to: all plant material is to be delivered in closed and, if necessary, temperature-controlled vehicles to prevent damage to the foliage; plant material shipped in boxes must be opened immediately upon arrival; all plant material is to be stored and stockpiled to prevent damage to foliage; and no plant shall be bound with rope or wire in a manner that would damage the bark or break the branches.

04 PLANTING OPERATIONS:

A. Preparation: All plant beds shall be free of trash,

building materials, etc., before filling plant beds.

B. Planting: The contractor is responsible for planting all material at correct grades and alignment. All plants shall be set so that when settled they will bear the same relation to finish grade as they did before being transplanted. No filling will be permitted around trunks and stems. When the plant has been properly set, the pit shall be backfilled with planting mixture, gradually filling, tamping, and settling with water. The contractor shall make adjustments in the location of plants and planters where necessary as directed by the landscape architect. Additional plant material and planters not located on the plans, but included in the plant list, will be used as infill where necessary under the direction of the landscape architect.

C. Watering: All plants shall be thoroughly soaked after planting.

D. Pruning and Repair: Upon completion of planting, all trees and shrubs shall be pruned and have injuries repaired. The amount of pruning shall be limited to the minimum necessary to remove dead or injured twigs and branches and to compensate for the loss of roots from transplanting. Pruning shall be done in such a manner as not to change the natural habit or shape of the plant.

05 PROTECTION:
The contractor shall protect all plants from damage at all times. If the plants are damaged, they should be replaced or treated by the contractor at his or her own expense to the satisfaction of the landscape architect.

06 WATERING AND MAINTENANCE:
The contractor shall assume responsibility for maintaining the work to the end of the guarantee period. During this period, the contractor shall make a minimum

of one maintenance trip every two weeks, and as many more as necessary to keep the plants in a thriving condition. Written reports of maintenance trips shall be submitted to the landscape architect.

07 ACCEPTANCE:

At the end of the period of guarantee, final acceptance will be made by the landscape architect and the representative of the owner, provided all requirements of the specifications have been fulfilled.

08 GUARANTEE:

A. Time Period: The contractor agrees to guarantee all plants for three months from completion of planting, which must comply with the owner's "date of completion." The owner will supply this date. This guarantee includes furnishing new plants as well as labor and materials for installation of replacements. All replacements shall be guaranteed and maintained for an additional period of three months. Any tree 5″ (12.7 cm) or over in caliper shall be guaranteed for six months. Replacement stock must meet specifications and quality of original stock. At the end of the three- and six-month guarantee periods, the contractor shall submit for final acceptance.

B. Reponsibility: The contractor shall not assume responsibility for damages or loss of plants or trees caused by fire, pedestrian traffic, and vandalism.

C. Inspection: Inspection of the planting will be made jointly by the contractor and landscape architect at the completion of planting. All plants not in a healthy, growing condition shall be removed and replaced with plants of like kind, size, and quality as originally specified.

4/DESIGN ENCYCLOPEDIA

The following is a general list of the more popular foliage materials used in interior landscapes. It includes 90 genera and over 475 species presented as a reference resource.

A brief *description* of each plant's major growth characteristics as well as its family origin are provided. The *culture* information includes light, temperature, moisture, and humidity averages. When insects or diseases are a major design problem, they too are listed. The *design application* is for general consideration only. The more creative the designer, the greater the range of uses the plants will have. (Appendix B lists other plants that may be used in the interior landscape.)

NAME:

Abutilon (ab-yew-til-on)

DESCRIPTION:

A member of the mallow family (Malvaceae) and a native of Brazil. It is related to the Chinese hibiscus. Reaches an average height of 36″ (.9 m), but may grow to 10′ (3 m) in special situations. Leaves are lobed and dark green and grow on long stalks. Flowers (yellow) are bellshaped, drooping, and everblooming. It grows rapidly and needs repotting often. Does not follow a symmetrical pattern of growth—more irregular.

CULTURE:

Light, sunny to semisunny. Temperature, 60° F (16° C) to 72° F (22° C). Humidity, 40% to 50%. Needs good air circulation. Standard soil mix. Keep soil evenly moist. Subject to mealybugs, whiteflies, scale, mites.

DESIGN APPLICATION:

Specimen plant in individual planter. Showy flowers.

SPECIES:

A. megapotamicum (Flowering Maple, Parlor Maple), *A. m. variegata, A. striatum* (orange flower), *A. s. Thompsonii* (green yellow variegated leaves).

NAME:

Acalypha (ah-kaa-lee-fa)

DESCRIPTION:

A member of the spurge family (Euphorbiaceae) native to Burma and the East Indies. Usually grows to a height of 3′ (.9 m), but may reach greater heights if used as a specimen plant. Has colorful, crimson and bronze, ornate leaves. Has showy, drooping flower spikes. Used both inside and outside. Often called Copperplant.

CULTURE:

Light, bright (full sun). Keep soil evenly moist. Can tolerate temperatures above 70° F (21° C). Humidity, above 45%. Needs good air circulation. Standard soil mix with extra peat. Crowds easily. Subject to mealybugs and scale.

DESIGN APPLICATION:

Accent specimen. Border or mass for color. Not recommended for hanging baskets. Groundcovers, small shrubs.

SPECIES:

A. hispida (Chenille Plant), *A. h. Alba* (white flowers), *A. wilkesiana* (Beefsteak Plant), *A. w. Macafeana* (Copper Leaf).

NAME:

Achimenes (ah-kim-en-eez)

DESCRIPTION:

A member of the gesneriad family (Gesneriaceae) from tropical America. Has numerous hybrids. Generally, the growth habit is low (no more than 12″ to 14″) (30.4 to 35.5 cm). The tubular blossoms are similar to petunia and are found in reds, violet, purple, and blue (some are solid, others may be veined or spotted). The leaves are elmlike. The foliage glistens, is hairy, and ranges from pale green to reddish bronze.

CULTURE:

Light, semisunny to semishady, southern exposure in winter. Temperature, 65° F (18° C) to 75° F (23° C) or higher. Will go dormant around mid-October if used outdoors; variable when used in full enclosure. Keep the soil evenly moist at the roots.

DESIGN APPLICATION:

Short periods for accent masses with showy flowers. Groundcover.

SPECIES:

A. andrieuxii (small, violet flowers), *A. antirrhina* (scarlet and yellow flowers), *A. candida* (pure white flowers), *A. ehrenbergii* (orchid flowers), *A. erecta* (scarlet flowers), *A. flava* (golden yellow flowers), *A. grandiflora* (large flowers, purple), *A. pedunculata* (orange flowers).

NAME:

Acorus (ah-kor-us)

DESCRIPTION:

A member of the arum family (Araceae) from Japan. Reaches height of 12″ (30.4 cm). It has flat, grasslike, green, stiff leaves in fan-shaped tufts. Its roots are used in making perfume; the plant has a lemon-scented fragrance.

CULTURE:

Light, bright, indirect or curtain-filtered sunlight. Will tolerate temperatures from 40° F (4° C) to 80° F (26° C). Humidity, 60% to 70%. Soil should be kept thoroughly moist. Air circulation should be moderate.

DESIGN APPLICATION:

Small accent features, specimen when used three to four plants at a time, or terrariums. Groundcovers.

SPECIES:

A. gramineus 'Variegatus' (cream-striped leaves), *A. calamus* (Sweet Flag, variegated foliage), *A. g. pusillus* (miniature).

NAME:

Adiantum (ad-ee-an-tum)

DESCRIPTION:

A member of the fern family (Polypodiaceae) and originally from Brazil. Reaches height of 4' (1.2 m). Fronds are feathery, triangular in shape, wedgelike. Dark green color.

CULTURE:

North window exposure is best. Temperature, 50° F (10° C) to 75° F (23° C). Humidity, very high (usually 70%). Damaged easily if touched often. Needs good air circulation, but avoid drafts. Soil, standard with extra peat. Roots often cling to the walls of the planter, so caution should be taken when moving. Mist often. Subject to mealybugs, aphids, thrips, and red spiders.

DESIGN APPLICATION:

Fine-textured masses, hanging baskets, small accents.

SPECIES:

A. capillus-veneris (Southern Maidenhair Fern), *A. caudatum* (Trailing Maidenhair Fern), *A. hispidulum* (Rosy Maidenhair Fern), *A. pedatum* (American Maidenhair Fern), *A. tenerum* (Brittle Maidenhair Fern).

4-1. *Adiantum capillus veneris.*

NAME:

Adromischus (ad-ro-misk-us)

DESCRIPTION:

A member of the stonecrop family (Crassulaceae) from South Africa. The growth habit is small (close to the soil), usually not more than 2″ to 3″ (5 to 7.6 cm) high. Its foliage is found in all shades of green; many have accents of red and purple. The leaves are thick and fleshy. Its flowers are very small, not showy.

CULTURE:

Light, can withstand direct sun for short periods (4 to 6 hours). Temperature, 50° F (10° C) to 80° F (26° C). Humidity, low to around 20% to 25%. Needs air circulation. Standard soil, with extra sand. Allow soil to become quite dry before watering. Subject to scale, mealybugs, and root rot from overwatering.

DESIGN APPLICATION:

Small (short) masses, groundcovers.

SPECIES:

A. clavifolius (Pretty Pebbles), *A. cooperi*, *A. cristatus* (Sea Shells), *A. festivus* (Plover Eggs), *A. hemisphaericus*, *A. maculatus* (Calico Hearts).

NAME:

Aechmea (ah-ch-me-a)

DESCRIPTION:

A member of the pineapple family (Bromeliaceae) from Brazil. The flowers bloom in various seasons and are longlasting. The leaf rosettes are variable in color, light green to variegated with purple, and are able to hold water. Subject to injury.

CULTURE:

Light, sunny to semisunny. Temperature range, 50° F (10° C) to 80° F (26° C). Humidity, 50% or higher. Use standard soil, but add extra humus. Water roots sparingly. Avoid cold-air drafts.

DESIGN APPLICATION:

Masses if planted close, specimen in decorative planter, accent shrubs.

SPECIES:

A. fasciata silver vase.

4-2. *Aechmea fasciata.*

NAME:

Aeschynanthus (esk-in-an-thus)

DESCRIPTION:

A member of the gesneriad family (Gesneriaceae) from Java. Reaches height of 2' (.6 m) or more. Brilliant red tubular flowers. Trailing or climbing stems. Dark green, glossy, fleshy leaves. Flower buds resemble lipstick.

CULTURE:

Light, semisunny to semishady. Temperature, 65° F (18° C) to 75° F (23° C). Humidity, moist air, around 70%. Keep soil evenly moist at all times. Needs good air circulation.

DESIGN APPLICATION:

Accent, good in hanging baskets.

SPECIES:

A. marmoratus (Zebra Basketvine), *A. pulcher* (Royal Red Bugler), *A. Pullobia*, *A. speciosus*.

NAME:

Agapanthus (ag-a-pan-thus)

DESCRIPTION:

Large, tuberous-rooted, summer-flowering. Member of the lily family (Liliaceae) from Africa. Reaches height of 3' (.9 m). Leathery-textured leaves are narrow and thick, and may reach 2' (.6 m) in length.

CULTURE:

Light, sunny to semishady. Temperature, 50° F (10° C) to 72° F (22° C). Humidity, in the range of 40% to 50%. Use standard soil mix; do not allow to dry out. Mist often. Will become potbound easily. Subject to mealybugs, scale, thrips.

DESIGN APPLICATION:

Accent specimens, showy masses.

SPECIES:

A. campanulatus; A. hybrids: peter pan, dwarf white; A. inapertus; A. pendulus.

NAME:

Agave (ah-gaa-vee)

DESCRIPTION:

The true succulent, member of the amaryllis family (Amaryllidaceae) from Mexico and Central America. Basically a tough plant 3' to 4' (.9 to 1.2 m) in height. Foliage is fleshy, stiff, sword-shaped, in rosettes. Does not flower often indoors, but when it does it is very attractive.

CULTURE:

Light, sunny (often full sun). Temperature, from 50° F (10° C) to 80° F (26° C). Will tolerate low humidity to 25%. Needs air circulation. Allow sandy soil to become dry between waterings. Mist lightly. Subject to scale and mealybugs. Leaves will develop brown spots from excessive heat or high humidity.

DESIGN APPLICATION:

Specimen in single container (tub).

SPECIES:

A. americana (gray-green leaves), *A. a. Marginata* (yellow-edged leaves), *A. filifera* (bright olive leaves), *A. picta* (variegated), *A. victoriae reginae* (Queen Victoria Century Plant).

NAME:
Aglaonema (ag-la-o-nee-ma)

DESCRIPTION:
One of the hardiest of interior plants, it is a member of the arum family (Araceae) from Indonesia, Malaya, and Africa. A tough plant to 4′ (1.2 m) with dark green to silvery leaves, arrow shaped, 2″ (5 cm) to 6″ (15.2 cm) wide. Tiny flowers; not showy when it does bloom.

CULTURE:
Light, semishady to shady. Temperature, 62° F (16° C) to 80° F (26° C). Humidity, 45% to 55%. Use standard soil; do not allow it to become too dry. Mist often. Needs good air circulation for best effect. Subject to mealybugs, red spiders, scale, thrips, and aphids.

DESIGN APPLICATION:
Shrub mass, small specimen.

SPECIES:
A. commutatum, A. costatum, A. crispum, A. modestum, A. pseudobracteatum, A. roebelinii, A. treubii.

4-4. *Aglaonema pseudobracteatum.*
(Courtesy, Tropical Ornamentals)

4-3. *Aglaonema costatum.*
(Courtesy, Tropical Ornamentals)

4-5. *Aglaonema commutatum.*
(Courtesy, Tropical Ornamentals)

NAME:

Allamanda (al-lam-man-da)

DESCRIPTION:

A rapid-growing vine in the dogbane family (Apocynaceae) from Brazil. Can reach a height of 15′ (4.5 m). It has large, dark green, glossy, tubular leaves. Young leaves are pliable; older ones are brittle. Flowers are trumpet-shaped and golden yellow. Very showy plant in the right location.

CULTURE:

Light, sunny. Temperature, from 60° F (15° C) to 80° F (26° C). Humidity, to 50%. Keep standard (well-drained) soil moist. Mist often. Needs good air circulation. Subject to mealybugs, scale, whiteflies, and red mites.

DESIGN APPLICATION:

Hanging baskets.

SPECIES:

A. cathartica Hendersonii (large flowers), *A. neriifolia* (yellow-streaked flowers), *A. violacea* (violet color).

NAME:

Allophyton (al-low-phy-ton)

DESCRIPTION:

A member of the figwort family (Scrophulariaceae) from Mexico and Guatemala. Reaches a height of 12″ (30.4 cm). Dark green, compact leaves in a rosette; leathery; to 5″ (12.7 cm) in length. Flower stalks are from the center of the plant; pink to purple.

CULTURE:

Light, semisunny to semishady. Temperatures, from 60° F (15° C) to 72° F (22° C). Humidity, 50% to 60%. Keep standard soil evenly moist. Provide good air circulation. Subject to aphids, mites, scale, and mealybugs.

SPECIES:

A. mexicanum (Mexican Foxglove).

NAME:

Aloe (al-o)

DESCRIPTION:

A member of the lily family (Liliaceae) from South Africa. Reaches height of 2′ (.6 m). Has thick, fleshy, tender leaves that form rosettes. Some varieties have spotted leaves; some are plain. Leaf edges range from smooth to spiny.

CULTURE:

Light, sunny to semisunny. Temperatures should range from 50° F (10° C) to 80° F (26° C). Tolerates a low humidity to 25%. Allow a sandy soil to become dry before watering. Subject to scale, mealybugs, and root rot from overwatering.

DESIGN APPLICATION:

Small accent. Small mass if crowded.

SPECIES:

A. arborescens (Tree Aloe), *A. aristata* (slender leaves), *A. brevifolia* (shortleaved), *A. ciliaris* (Crocodile Aloe), *A. nobilis* (Gold-toothed Aloe), *A. variegata* (Pheasant Wing Aloe), *A. vera* (True Aloe).

4-6. *Aloe vera.*

4-7. *Aloe vera.*

NAME:

Amaryllis (am-a-rill-us)

DESCRIPTION:

A member of the amaryllis family (Amaryllidaceae) from South America. Reaches height of 3' (.9 m). Its leaves are dark green and star shaped on stout stalks. The flowers are smooth, trumpet shaped, and lilylike.

CULTURE:

Light, semishady. Temperature, 60° F (15° C) to 70° F (21° C) or higher. Standard soil should be kept evenly moist. Mist lightly, daily. Good air movement is helpful. Plant as bulbs. Keep out of direct sunlight when blooming. Flower stalk will need support. Subject to mealybugs, red spiders, and bulb flies.

DESIGN APPLICATION:

Accent specimens in containers or mixed into masses of other material.

SPECIES:

A. belladonna elata (rosy flowers), *A. b. alba.*

NAME:

Ananas (a-nan-as)

DESCRIPTION:

A member of the pineapple family (Bromeliaceae) from tropical America. Grows to 3′ (.9 m) in height. Narrow, gray green, variegated, sharp-edged leaves. Flowers are purple with pink, red, and white bracts on long stalks. After several years of proper habitat, the fruit (pineapple) may develop.

4-8. *Ananas comosus.*

CULTURE:

Light, tolerant to full sun. Temperature, 60° F (15° C) to 85° F (29° C). Humidity, 50% to 60%. Soil should be a special mix (tree fern mixture). Water thoroughly, but do not allow soil to become soaked. Subject to scale and thrips; leaves yellow from too much direct sun or when temperature is too cool.

DESIGN APPLICATION:

Small specimen.

SPECIES:

A. comosus (Pineapple).

NAME:

Anthurium (an-thur-e-um)

DESCRIPTION:

A member of the arum family (Araceae) from Central and South America. Dark green, drooping, glossy foliage. Showy, flowerlike spathes. Some species are grown for their attractive foliage, others strictly for their flowers. Growth habits vary from vining, self-heading, treelike, to shrubby. Some varieties cling well to rocks.

CULTURE:

Light, semishady. Temperature, 65° F (18° C) to 85° F (29° C). Humidity, over 70%. Keep standard soil evenly moist. Mist often. Sensitive root system. Will not do well in artificial light. Subject to red spiders, mites, mealybugs, whiteflies, and scale. To 2′ (.6 m) in height.

DESIGN APPLICATION:

Small masses, borders, or accent mass.

SPECIES:

A. andraeanum, A. caribbeum, A. clarinervium, A. forgetii (oval leaves), *A. scandens* (dark green climber), *A. warocqueanum* (velvety climber), *A. veitchii* (metallic green leaves).

4-9. *Anthurium andraeanum.*
(Courtesy, Tropical Ornamentals)

4-10. *Anthurium caribbeum.*
(Courtesy, Tropical Ornamentals)

4-11. *Anthurium clarinervium.*
(Courtesy, Tropical Ornamentals)

NAME:

Aphelandra (ah-phe-lan-dra)

DESCRIPTION:

A member of the acanthus family (Acanthaceae) from Brazil. Reaches height of 3' (.9 m). Its leaves are large and fleshy; range from gray green to dark green with white veins. Flower colors are mostly orange scarlet or yellow and very showy.

CULTURE:

Light, semisunny. Temperature, 65° F (18° C) to 75° F (23° C). Humidity, 65% or higher. Standard soil should be kept thoroughly and evenly moist. Mist daily. Needs good air circulation. Subject to scale and whiteflies; rolled leaf edges and brown spot from too-dry air.

DESIGN APPLICATION:

Good groundcover mass for both flower and foliage color.

SPECIES:

A. chamissoniana (popular Zebra Plant), *A. squarrosa* (yellow flowers), *A. s. Leopoldii* (orange flowers), *A. s. Dania* (tolerates lower temperatures), *A. s. Louisae* (bright veins), *A. tetragona* (tubular scarlet flowers).

NAME:

Aralia (ah-rail-ee-a)

A group of fast-growing evergreen plant materials commonly used in the exterior landscape. The interior *Aralias* are made up of species from *Dizygotheca* (commonly called False Aralias) and *Polyscias*. See *Dizygotheca*.

NAME:

Araucaria (air-a-care-e-a)

DESCRIPTION:

A member of the araucaria family (Araucariaceae) from South America. Reaches height of 20′ (6 m) or more; best when averaging 12′ to 15′ (3.6 to 4.5 m). May produce cones to 6″ (15.2 cm). It has glossy green foliage that branches in the form of a true pine tree (which it is not). Withstands people blight. Very attractive evergreen.

CULTURE:

Light, semisunny to semishady. Likes cool temperatures, 40° F (4° C) to 65° F (18° C). Humidity, 30% to 35%. Needs good air circulation. Standard soil should be watered evenly and thoroughly; allow to dry between waterings. Subject to aphids, mealybugs, mites, scale, and leaf miners.

DESIGN APPLICATION:

Good canopy when large. Baffle. Multitrunk makes an excellent specimen.

SPECIES:

A. araucana (Monkey Puzzle Tree), *A. bidwillii* (bunya Bunya Tree), *A. excelsa* (Norfolk Island Pine).

4-12. *Araucaria excelsa.*

4-13. *Araucaria excelsa.*

NAME:

Ardisia (ar-diz-e-ah)

DESCRIPTION:

A well-known evergreen from Malaya, China, and the East Indies, and a member of the myrsine family (Myrsinaceae). Reaches height of 4′ (1.2 m). Leaves are long, thick, glossy, and margined. Flowers are small, white, and fragrant. It makes a graceful small tree—almost hollylike.

CULTURE:

Light, semisunny to semishady. Temperature, 50° F (10° C) to 72° F (22° C). Humidity, at least 50%. Keep standard soil evenly moist. Mist often. Good air circulation is important.

DESIGN APPLICATION:

Shrub to small tree in masses. Large plant for specimen.

SPECIES:

A. crispa (Coral Berry), *A. japonica* (white berries).

NAME:

Asparagus (ah-spare-ah-gus)

DESCRIPTION:

A member of the lily family (Liliaceae) from Africa. Can reach 3′ (.9 m) in a mound shape. Stems are arching and covered with small, bright green, needlelike leaves. Flowers are small, pinkish, and hot; always prominent. Very attractive fine texture.

CULTURE:

Light, semisunny to shady. Temperature, 50° F (10° C) to 72° F (22° C). Humidity, 30% to 35%. Keep standard soil evenly moist. Mist often.

DESIGN APPLICATION:

Low shrub mass, plant close.

SPECIES:

A. asparagoides (small oval leaves), *A. falcatus* (long leaves, in clusters), *A. meyersii* (Foxtail Asparagus), *A. myriocladus*, *A. plumosus*, *A. retrofractus* (Twisted Asparagus Fern), *A. sprengeri*.

4-14. *Asparagus sprengeri.*

4-15. *Asparagus sprengeri.*

NAME:

Aspidistra (ass-pa-dis-tra)

DESCRIPTION:

This member of the lily family (Liliaceae) from China takes abuse (people blight) very well. Generally reaches 3′ (.9 m) but can be larger under forced conditions. Its lance-shaped, green leaves droop in an attractive pattern. Flowers are not dominant.

4-16. *Aspidistra elatior.*

CULTURE:

Light, semishady to shady. Temperature, to the cool side, 50° F (10° C) to 68° F (20° C). Humidity, 30% to 40%. Use standard soil mix; water moderately. Good in artificial light. Very tough plant. Subject to scale.

DESIGN APPLICATION:

Good specimen. Medium height mass if planted close.

SPECIES:

A. elatior (Cast Iron Plant), *A. e. variegata* (white/green striped leaves).

NAME:

Asplenium (ass-plen-e-um)

DESCRIPTION:

A member of the common fern family (Polypodiaceae) from Asia. Its leaves (fronds) vary with different species.

CULTURE:

Light, semisunny to semishady. Humidity, 60% to 70%. Add extra peat moss to a standard soil mix, which should never be allowed to dry out. Mist daily. Avoid direct drafts of air. Subject to mealybugs, aphids, thrips, and red spiders.

DESIGN APPLICATION:

Small specimen in groups of two to three. Mass requires close planting.

SPECIES:

A. bulbiferum (Mother's Fern, long, bright green, divided fronds that produce bulbs), *A. nidus* (Bird's Nest Fern, bright green fronds in a rosette), *A. platyneuron* (Ebony Spleenwort, low-growing frond with dark brown stems), *A. trichomanes* (Maidenhair Spleenwort, small, thick-clustered fronds).

4-17. *Asplenium nidus.*
(Courtesy, Tropical Ornamentals)

NAME:
Aucuba (ah-koo-ba)

DESCRIPTION:
This attractive evergreen is a member of the dogwood family (Cornaceae) from Japan. It reaches a height of 15' (4.5 m). Has long, waxy green leaves with toothed margins. Some varieties have gold-specked or green-edged leaves.

CULTURE:
Light, semishady (do not place in direct sunlight). Temperature, 40° F (4° C) to 78° F (25° C). Humidity, 30% to 40%. Standard soil mix should be allowed to dry before watering evenly. Mist often. Good air circulation is important. Subject to aphids, mealybugs, mites, scale, leaf miners.

DESIGN APPLICATION:
Small to medium shrub mass. Small specimen tree.

SPECIES:
A. japonica (Japanese Aucuba), *A. j. 'Variegata'* (Variegated Aucuba), *A. j. 'Picturata'* (yellow-centered leaves).

NAME:

Beaucarnea (bo-kar-nee-ah)

DESCRIPTION:

Member of the lily family (Liliaceae) from Mexico and South Africa. Older plants may reach height of 30′ (9 m). It has sturdy leaves that may reach 4′ (1.2 m) in length and 1″ (2.5 cm) in width. It is noted primarily for its large, swollen base, giving it the name of Bottle Plant or Pony Tail Plant. Its flowers are small, white, and fragrant.

CULTURE:

Light, sunny to semisunny. Temperature, 55° F (12° C) to 80° F (26° C). Humidity, 40% to 45%. Let standard soil become slightly dry before watering. Mist often. Good air circulation is important. Subject to mealybugs, whiteflies, mites, scale, and slugs. Dust will inhibit plant quality.

DESIGN APPLICATION:

Specimen. Best in small decorative pots as single or multiple plant.

SPECIES:

B. recurvata (green leaves).

4-18. *Beaucarnea recurvata.*

NAME:

Begonia (bi-go-nee-ah)

DESCRIPTION:

This large group of succulent herbs (Begoniaceae) is native to tropical America and Asia. They are grouped, generally, according to the following classifications:

1. *Wax Begonias*: The fibrous-rooted begonias, which have many compact branches with almost round, waxy green leaves.

2. *Cane Stems*: The fibrous-rooted begonias with lopsided leaves shaped like "angel wings."

3. *Hairy-leaved Begonias*: Mostly fibrous rooted, with leaves coated with velvety hair.

4. *Rhizomatous Begonias*: Have a ground-level stem that creeps along the ground and sends down shallow roots.

5. *Rex Begonias*: Grown mostly for their foliage of bright colors and patterns.

6. *Tuberous Begonias*: The summer flowering maple-leaf species.

CULTURE:

Light, sunny to semishady. Temperature, 58° F (14° C) to 75° F (23° C). Humidity, 30% to 35%. Allow soil mix (1 part loam, 2 parts peat for tuberous and rhizomatous; 1 part loam, 1 part sand, 1 part peat for fibrous) to dry between waterings. Subject to mealybugs, slugs, whiteflies, scale, and mildew.

DESIGN APPLICATION:

Specimen masses for bright accents.

NAME:

Beloperone (bell-o-per-o-nee)

DESCRIPTION:

A member of the acanthus family (Acanthaceae) from tropical America. Reaches a height of 3′ (.9 m). It is a wiry-stemmed plant that needs trimming often. The leaves are oval and outlined in dark red coloring. Flowers are shaped like a small shrimp—thus the name Shrimp Plant.

CULTURE:

Light, sunny or semisunny. Temperature, 50° F (10° C) to 72° F (22° C). Humidity, above 45%. Standard soil should be allowed to become slightly dry between waterings. Needs good air circulation. Subject to whiteflies and aphids. When soil is too dry, leaves will wilt and drop off. Too little light causes top leaves to wilt.

DESIGN APPLICATION:

Specimen plant in container.

SPECIES:

B. comosa (Red King, red leaves), *B. guttata* (Yellow Queen, yellow green).

NAME:

Bertolonia (ber-to-lon-nee-ah)

DESCRIPTION:

A member of the meadow-beauty family (Melastomaceae) from Brazil. Grows up to 9″ to 10″ (22.8 to 25.4 cm) in height. It has brown, oval leaves that are margined in red and completely covered with long hairs. All of the species in this genus have distinctively colored leaf veins. The flowers are small and produced on erect stems.

CULTURE:

Light, semishady to shady. Temperature, 65° F (18° C) to 75° F (23° C) (should be kept even if possible). Humidity, 50% to 60%. Standard soil should be kept evenly moist. The leaves will turn brown at the tips if the humidity is low and if there is too much direct sunlight. This is a very difficult plant to use in an interior landscape.

DESIGN APPLICATION:

Groundcover mass. Color accent mass.

SPECIES:

B. maculata, B. pubescens.

NAME:

Billbergia (bill-ber-gee-ah)

DESCRIPTION:

This member of the pineapple family (Bromeliaceae) is originally from Southern Brazil. It is grown primarily for its showy flowers, which grow in clusters on tall, drooping spikes. The bracts of the flowers often compete in color with flowers. Plants reach the height of 1' to 3' (.3 to .9 m). The leaves are stiff and grow in basal clusters.

CULTURE:

Light, sunny to semisunny. Temperature, 65° F (18° C) to 75° F (23° C). Humidity, 50% to 60%. Standard soil mix should be supplemented with sphagnum moss or charcoal. The root system should be in a medium that will hold moisture but will provide good aeration. The root system also has a tendency to be weak.

DESIGN APPLICATION:

Specimen in small pot. If the root system can be wrapped in sphagnum moss, this plant can be planted onto a large piece of bark or a tree limb for added accent effect.

SPECIES:

B. amoena, B. iridifolia conocolor, B. nutaus, B. pyramidalis, B. sanderana, B. venezueleana, B. zebrina.

NAME:

Bougainvillea (boo-gan-vill-e-ah)

DESCRIPTION:

This four-o'clock family member (Nyctaginaceae) is from Brazil. Its foliage is small and lance shaped. The color of the leaves is medium green and the stems are thorny. The flowers are tiny within three bracts. These plants are divided into those that climb and those that are erect.

CULTURE:

Light, sunny. Temperature, 60° F (15° C) to 80° F (26° C). Humidity, 45% to 50%. Standard soil should be kept evenly moist. Mist often. Air circulation is good for flowering. Subject to mealybugs and scale.

DESIGN APPLICATION:

Specimen mass (vine) as a vertical accent climber.

SPECIES:

B. glabra (hairless, smooth), *B. harrisii* (green and white leaves), *B. spectabilis* (vigorous grower).

NAME:

Brassaia (brass-sa-e-ah)

DESCRIPTION:

This member of the aralia family (Araliaceae) is from Australia. Reaches a height of 15′ (4.5 m). It has shiny green, oval leaves composed of 6 to 8 leaflets. The flowers are small and rarely bloom in the interior landscape.

CULTURE:

Light, sunny to shady. Temperature, 62° F (16° C) to 80° F (26° C). Humidity, 45% to 55%. Good air circulation is important. Standard soil should be watered thoroughly and should be allowed to dry between waterings. Mist daily. Subject to mealybugs, red spiders, scales, thrips, and aphids.

DESIGN APPLICATION:

Canopy, baffle.

SPECIES:

B. actinophylla (also known as *Schefflera actinophylla*).

4-19. *Brassaia actinophylla.*

NAME:

Buxus (book-sus)

DESCRIPTION:

This member of the box family (Buxaceae) is from Europe, North Africa, and Asia. It will reach a height of about 4' (1.2 m). Its small and shiny leaves, which are about 1/2" (1.1 cm) long, are deep evergreen. The very small flowers rarely bloom in the interior landscape.

CULTURE:

Light, sunny. Temperature, 50° F (10° C) to 75° F (23° C). Humidity, 45% to 55%. Standard soil should be allowed to dry between waterings. Subject to mealybugs, red spiders, scale, thrips, aphids, and leaf miners. Tolerates cool drafts of air better than most plants.

DESIGN APPLICATION:

Barrier. Use in close planted masses.

SPECIES:

B. sempervirens

NAME:

Caladium (ca-lay-dee-um)

DESCRIPTION:

This member of the arum family (Araceae) is originally from Brazil. The interior landscape varieties are numerous, and most have delicate, veined and patterned leaves. The colors range from green through red, purple, and white. The foliage is heart, lance, or arrow shaped, with color accents along the ribs. The flowers are quite small and generally concealed by the foliage. Flower sizes range from 2″ (5 cm) to 2′ (.6 m) in height.

CULTURE:

Light, semisunny to semishady. Temperature, 65° F (18° C) to 80° F (26° C). Humidity, 45% to 50%. Soil should be heavy in peat moss and should be kept constantly moist but not soggy.

DESIGN APPLICATION:

Accent, color masses, groundcover.

SPECIES:

C. bicolor (two-color leaf), *C. humboldtii* (Miniature).

NAME:

Calathea (ca-lath-ee-ah)

DESCRIPTION:

A member of the arrowroot family (Marantaceae) from South America. Reaches 2' (.6 m) in height. It is a member of a large group of highly decorative foliage plants. Its leaves are in tufts, broad, long, and have pointed tips, patterned with deep colorations. It does not flower often in cultivation.

CULTURE:

Light, semishady. Temperature, 60° F (15° C) to 85° F (29° C). Humidity, 45% to 50%. Standard soil should be kept evenly moist, but not soggy. Subject to mealybugs, red spiders, scale, thrips, and aphids.

DESIGN APPLICATION:

Color accent, groundcover mass.

SPECIES:

C. bachemiana (gray green leaves), *C. illustris* (olive green leaves), *C. leopardina* (waxy green leaves), *C. lietzei* (light green leaves), *C. picturata*, *C. p. argentea* (dwarf, silvered leaves), *C. roseo-picta* (red mid-rib), *C. vandenheckei* (white/dark green), *C. zebrina* (Zebra Plant), *C. z. binotii*.

NAME:

Calceolaria (cal-ce-o-la-ree-ah)

DESCRIPTION:

A member of the snapdragon family (Scrophulariaceae) from South America (Chile and Peru). It may reach 2′ (.6 m) in height. Large foliage, sometimes to 6″ (15.2 cm), is soft and covered with hairs. The dark green color of its leaves helps to contrast the dominant, attractive foliage.

CULTURE:

Light, sunny to semisunny. Temperature, 50° F (10° C) to 70° F (21° C). Humidity, above 45%. Keep the standard soil mix evenly moist. Mist often. Avoid drafts and high temperatures. Subject to slugs, aphids, red spider mites, whiteflies, and gray mold.

DESIGN APPLICATION:

Small specimen plant.

SPECIES:

C. arachnoidea (small purple flowers), *C. crenatiflora*, *C. herbeohybrida* (bushy, compact), *C. multiflora nana* (dwarf), *C. rugosa* (wrinkled leaves).

NAME:
Callisia (cal-lee-see-ah)

DESCRIPTION:
A member of the spiderwort family (Commelinaceae) from Mexico. Reaches 3' (.9 m) in size. It has striped, green and white foliage with purple undersides.

CULTURE:
Light, semisunny, semishady. Temperature, 55° F (12° C) to 80° F (26° C). Humidity, 40% to 45%. Add extra peat moss and perlite to standard soil mix, and keep evenly moist. Mist often. Subject to mealybugs, whiteflies, mites, scale, and slugs. Do not overwater because of rot susceptibility. Overfeeding may cause discoloration of leaves.

DESIGN APPLICATION:
Groundcover mass. Hanging basket.

SPECIES:
C. elegans (Striped Inch Plant).

NAME:

Camellia (ca-meal-ee-ah)

DESCRIPTION:

A member of the tea family (Theaceae) from eastern Asia. Reaches height of 3′ (.9 m). Its leaves are oval, dark green, and glossy, and reach length of 4″ (10.1 cm). These species are well-known for their waxy, long-lasting blossoms.

CULTURE:

Light, sunny to semisunny. Temperature, 40° F (4° C) to 68° F (20° C). Humidity, 60% to 65%. Add extra humus and peat moss to a standard soil and keep constantly moist. Subject to scale, mealybugs, aphids, and mites. The buds drop off when the temperature is too high or too low. Avoid drafts.

DESIGN APPLICATION:

Accent specimen. Barrier mass.

SPECIES:

C. japonica, C. reticulata, C. sasanqua.

NAME:

Campanula (cam-pan-u-la)

DESCRIPTION:

A member of the bellflower family (Campanulaceae) from Europe and Asia. Reaches height of 2′ (.6 m). The gray green, oval leaves reach length of 1″ (2.5 cm) on trailing stems. The flowers are cup or star shaped on short stems.

CULTURE:

Light, sunny to semisunny. Temperature, 50° F (10° C) to 72° F (22° C). Humidity, 30% to 40%. Add extra peat moss and perlite to a standard soil mix. Subject to slugs, whiteflies, scale, and mealybugs. Leaves will drop off if soil is allowed to dry out.

DESIGN APPLICATION:

Specimen in small planter. Plant close together for mass.

SPECIES:

C. alba, C. elatines, C. fragilis, C. isophylla, C. mayii, C. poscharskyana.

NAME:

Capsicum (cap-si-cum)

DESCRIPTION:

A member of the nightshade family (Solanaceae) from tropical America. Reaches height of 5′ (1.5 m). Forms small shrubs of bright green leaves, oval in shape, to 2″ (5 cm) in length. The flowers are star shaped, tiny, and nondescript in detail. The fruit (for which it is known) displays several colors (green, white, yellow, red, and purple) at the same time. It will fruit when the plant is about six months old.

4-20. *Capsicum annuum.*

CULTURE:

Light, sunny to semisunny. Temperature, 60° F (15° C) to 72° F (22° C). Humidity, 35% to 40%. Standard soil should be kept evenly moist. Mist daily. Subject to whiteflies and aphids. Hot temperatures will cause the fruit to drop.

DESIGN APPLICATION:

Shrub masses. Do not place too close to people. Avoid access to fruit.

SPECIES:

C. annuum (Christmas Pepper), *C. a. acuminatum* (long peppers), *C. a. abbreviatum* (small ornamental), *C. a. cerasiforme* (Cherry Pepper).

NAME:

Carissa (car-riss-ah)

DESCRIPTION:

A member of the dogbane family (Apocynaceae) from South Africa. Reaches height of 5′ (1.5 m). Dwarf varieties reach 2′ (.6 m). It is fast growing and has glossy, dark green leaves to 3″ (7.6 cm) in length. The star shaped flowers are fragrant, white, and reach 2″ (5 cm) across. The fruit is reddish in color, about 2″ (5 cm) in size.

CULTURE:

Light, sunny to semisunny. Temperature, 50° F (10° C) to 72° F (22° C). Humidity, 50% to 55%. Standard soil mix should be kept evenly moist. Mist often. Subject to aphids, mealybugs, whiteflies, and scale. Wash leaves often for best results. Good air circulation is helpful.

DESIGN APPLICATION:

Specimen canopy in large planter. Small shrub mass (dwarf variety only).

SPECIES:

C. grandiflora, C. g. nana compacta.

NAME:

Caryota (car-ee-o-ta)

DESCRIPTION:

A member of the palm family (Palmaceae) from Asia. Reaches height of 10′ (3 m). Noted for its thin central trunk with numerous stems. The deep, rich green leaves resemble fish tails. Slow growing.

CULTURE:

Light, semisunny to semishady. Temperature, 58° F (14° C) to 75° F (23° C). Humidity, 45% to 60%. Standard soil mix should have extra peat moss and 1 part vermiculite; keep it evenly moist but allow it to dry between waterings. Good air circulation is necessary for top performance. Subject to mealybugs, red spiders, scale, and thrips. Do not place in drafts. Leaf pores should never be allowed to clog.

DESIGN APPLICATION:

Upright canopy, baffle. Excellent specimen tree.

SPECIES:

C. mitis, C. plumosa, C. urens.

NAME:

Ceropegia (cer-o-pee-gee-ah)

DESCRIPTION:

This tropical member of the milkweed family (Asclepiadaceae) is from Africa and Asia. It has heart shaped, succulent leaves that are silvery green on top and purple underneath. The purplish to pink flowers are about 1 1/2″ (3.8 cm) long and bottlelike in shape (often referred to as umbrellalike). The stems are trailing, reaching to 5′ (1.5 m) in length.

CULTURE:

Light, sunny to semishady. Temperature, 50° F (10° C) to 72° F (22° C). Humidity, 25% to 40%. Standard soil needs extra sand; allow to dry between thorough waterings. Mist lightly, regularly. Likes plenty of light. Subject to mites.

DESIGN APPLICATION:

Vine, hanging baskets.

SPECIES:

C. barkleyi (green leaves, silver markings), *C. caffrorum* (arrow shaped leaves), *C. debilis* (narrow green leaves), *C. fusca* (brown/yellow blooms), *C. haygarthii* (cream flowers), *C. radicans* (green, purple, white flowers), *C. sandersonii* (Parachute Plant), *C. stapeliiformis* (dark green leaves), *C. woodii* (Chinese Lantern Plant).

NAME:

Chamaedorea (cam-ee-do-ree-ah)

DESCRIPTION:

A member of the palm family (Palmaceae) from Mexico and South America. Reaches height of 10′ (3 m). The leaves (fronds) reach 3′ (7.6 m); they are deep green in color and reedlike in appearance.

CULTURE:

Light, semishady to shady. Temperature, 58° F (14° C) to 75° F (23° C). Humidity, 45% to 60%. The standard potting soil should have extra peat moss and 1 part vermiculite. Good air circulation is important. No drafts. Allow soil to dry between waterings. Subject to mealybugs, red spiders, scale, and thrips. Keep leaves clean.

DESIGN APPLICATION:

Specimen, baffle, canopy (more mature species).

SPECIES:

C. costaricana, *C. elegans* (Parlor Palm, this is the most adaptable of the species to the interior), *C. erumpens* (Bamboo Palm), *C. graminifolia*, *C. seifrizii* (lacy palm), *C. tenella* (dwarf).

4-21. *Chamaedorea erumpens*. (Courtesy, Tropical Ornamentals)

4-22. *Chamaedorea elegans*.

NAME:
Chamaerops (cam-ee-rops)

DESCRIPTION:
A member of the palm family (Palmaceae) from the Mediterranean area. In pots or planters, it may reach height of 10' (3 m). Its leaves are stiff and fan shaped, radiating from a central hair-covered trunk, and are dark green in color. Slow growing.

CULTURE:
Light, semishady to shady. Temperature, 58° F (14° C) to 75° F (23° C). Humidity, 45% to 60%. To a standard potting soil, add extra peat moss and vermiculite, and allow it to dry between waterings. Good air circulation is very important. Subject to mealybugs, red spiders, scale, and thrips. Clean leaves regularly.

DESIGN APPLICATION:
Baffle. Canopy (larger specimens).

Species:
C. humilis (European Fan Palm).

NAME:

Chlorophytum (clor-o-phy-tum)

DESCRIPTION:

A member of the lily family (Liliaceae) from South Africa. It may reach 3' (.9 m) across. It has long, narrow, grasslike leaves striped in yellow or white. The stems are long and cascade gracefully, with numerous plantlets.

4-23. *Chlorophytum comosum.*

CULTURE:

Light, semisunny to shady. Temperature, 60° F (15° C) to 75° F (23° C). Humidity, 30% to 40%. Standard soil mix should be allowed to dry between waterings. Mist often. Good air circulation is helpful. Subject to scale and people blight. Has a tendency to become asymmetrical.

DESIGN APPLICATION:

Baffle from a hanging cluster of pots. Specimen.

SPECIES:

C. bichetii (grassy green leaves), *C. comosum* (Airplane Plant), *C. c. mandaianum, C. c. picturatum, C. c. variegatum, C. c. vittatum, C. elatum.*

NAME:

Chrysalidocarpus (cris-al-ide-o-car-pus)

DESCRIPTION:

A member of the palm family (Palmaceae) from Madagascar. May reach 3′ to 5′ (.9 to 1.5 m) in size. It is small and graceful and has plume shaped leaves (fronds). The yellowish canes are in an arching clump. Slow growing.

CULTURE:

Light, semisunny to semishady. Temperature, 58° F (14° C) to 75° F (23° C). Humidity, 45% to 60%. Standard potting soil should have extra peat moss and 1 part vermiculite. Mist often. Good air circulation is essential to good design performance. No drafts. Subject to mealybugs, red spiders, scale, and thrips.

DESIGN APPLICATION:

Baffle. Specimen.

SPECIES:

C. lutescens (Madagascar Palm).

NAME:

Chrysanthemum (cris-san-thee-mum)

DESCRIPTION:

This member of the composite family (Compositae) is from China, Asia, and Europe. It has dark green leaves with slightly grayish undersides. Many stems come from a single base. A wide range of colors is available in daisylike shapes. Used primarily for its bloom.

CULTURE:

Light, sunny. Temperature, 40° F (4° C) to 60° F (15° C). Humidity, 35% to 40%. Keep standard soil evenly moist. Subject to aphids, thrips, and whiteflies. Leaves will yellow because of cold soil.

DESIGN APPLICATION:

Color accent, mass.

SPECIES:

C. frutescens (shrubby), *C. maximum* (Shasta Daisy), *C. morifolium* (Florist's Chrysanthemum), *C. parthenium*, *C. segetum* (Corn Marigold).

NAME:

Cissus (ciss-us)

DESCRIPTION:

This member of the grape family (Vitaceae) is from Australia, South America, and Asia. The stems may reach 5' (1.5 m). It has vining, trailing habits and its full-foliage characteristic makes it a popular ivy. Its leaves are heart shaped to oval in appearance and dark green to reddish in color.

4-24. *Cissus rhombifolia.*

CULTURE:

Light, semisunny to semishady. Temperature, 55° F (12° C) to 80° F (26° C). Humidity, 40% to 50%. Standard soil mix should be kept moderately and evenly moist. Subject to mealybugs, whiteflies, mites, scale, and brown spots (from high light intensity or overwatering). Wash foliage often.

DESIGN APPLICATION:

Baffle in hanging basket. Groundcover mass.

SPECIES:

C. adenopodus (velvety leaves), *C. antarctica* (kangaroo vine), *C. a. minima* (long leaves), *C. capensis, C. discolor, C. hypoglauca, C. incisa, C. quadrangula, C. rhombifolia* (Grape Ivy), *C. striata* (Miniature Grape Ivy).

NAME:

Citrus (sit-rus)

DESCRIPTION:

These are tropical shrubs and trees of the rue family (Rutaceae) from the Far East. Sizes to 15' (4.5 m). Used for their fruit and ornamentation. The foliage is dark green, shiny, oval shaped, and often aromatic. The flowers of most species are very fragrant. The fruit seldom develops in most interior landscapes, but is quite attractive and popular when it does.

CULTURE:

Light, sunny to semisunny. Temperature, 50° F (10° C) to 72° F (22° C). Humidity, 30% to 50%. Add extra humus to the standard potting soil, and allow the top portion of the soil to dry between waterings. Air circulation is helpful. Mist often. Subject to red spiders, scale, and mealybugs.

DESIGN APPLICATION:

Canopy. Specimen in large planter or tub.

SPECIES:

C. arantiifolia, *C. aurantium* (Sour Orange), *C. limonia* (Lemon), *C. l. meyeri*, *C. l. ponderosa*, *C. mitis*, *C. paradisi* (Tub Grapefruit), *C. reticulata*, *C. sinensis* (Sweet Orange), *C. taitensis* (Tahiti Orange).

NAME:

Coleus (co-lee-us)

DESCRIPTION:

This decorative member of the mint family (Labiatae) is from tropical Africa and Java. This very popular evergreen reaches a height of 4′ (1.2 m). The countless hybrids from this genus are erect plants with highly colored (full specimen) leaves that are generally oval with a point. The stems are succulent and erect. The flowers are erect and pale blue in color.

CULTURE:

Light, sunny (for best color) to semisunny. Temperature, 55° F (12° C) to 80° F (26° C). Humidity, 40% to 50%. Add extra peat moss and perlite to a standard soil mix; keep evenly moist. Mist often. Subject to mealybugs, whiteflies, mites, scale, and slugs. Older plants may develop root gall.

DESIGN APPLICATION:

Color masses for accent. Groundcover. Works well in hanging baskets.

SPECIES:

C. amboinicus, C. blumei, C. rehneltianus, C. thyrsoideus. (Due to the large number of colors and varieties of *Coleus*, it may be best to specify the color desired instead of the species.)

NAME:

Costus (cos-tus)

DESCRIPTION:

An aromatic herb of the ginger family (Zingiberaceae) from Central and South America. The foliage is shiny green, oval, with a pointed tip, and has a tendency to spiral. The flowers have edges that are rough and attractive. May reach 5′ (1.5 m) in height.

CULTURE:

Light, semisunny to semishady. Temperature, 55° F (12° C) to 80° F (26° C). Humidity, 40% to 50%. Standard soil should have extra peat moss and perlite. Mist often. Subject to mealybugs, whiteflies, scale, and slugs. Clean leaves often.

DESIGN APPLICATION:

Shrub mass when planted close together. Baffle.

SPECIES:

C. igneus (glossy green leaves, red undersides), *C. malortieanus* (Stepladder Plant), *C. sanguineus* (Spiral Flag), *C. speciosus* (Spiral Ginger).

NAME:

Crassula (crass-u-la)

DESCRIPTION:

Succulent, fleshy plants of the stonecrop family (Crassulaceae) from South Africa. Reaches to 4′ (1.2 m) in height. The foliage is rounded or oval and succulent. The stems are large and dominant in some species, hidden in others. The flowers are small and star shaped, and they range from white to pink.

4-25. *Crassula argentea.*

CULTURE:

Light, sunny to semisunny. Temperature, 62° F (16° C) to 80° F (26° C). Humidity, 30% to 40%. Standard potting soil should be allowed to dry between waterings. Mist daily. Subject to mealybugs, red spiders, scale, thrips, and aphids. Keep leaves clean. Avoid leaf shiners. Avoid people blight.

DESIGN APPLICATION:

Specimen plant.

SPECIES:

C. arborescens (Silver Dollar Plant), *C. argentea* (Jade Plant), *C. cooperi, C. corduta, C. falcata, C. lycopodioides* (Shoelace Plant), *C. perfoliata,C. rupestris, C. sarcocaulis, C. schmidtii.*

NAME:

Crocus (crow-cus)

DESCRIPTION:

This member of the iris family (Iridaceae) is from the Mediterranean area. It reaches 5″ to 6″ (12.7 to 15.2 cm) in height. The grasslike leaves are green with pronounced mid-ribs. The flowers are very showy and cup shaped, in a vivid range of colors.

CULTURE:

Light, sunny to semisunny. Temperature. 40° F (4° C) to 68° F (20° C). Humidity, 35% to 45%. Add extra perlite to standard soil mix, which should be kept evenly moist. Mist daily. Best when forced.

DESIGN APPLICATION:

Rotation specimen plants in mass. Accent specimens.

SPECIES:

(specify color desired): white, pink, lavender, purple, yellow, orange.

NAME:

Cycas (cy-cas)

DESCRIPTION:

A member of the cycas family (Cycadaceae) found in many of the tropical areas of the world. May reach 12′ (3.6 m) in height. It has stiff, dark green leaves growing from a central base, spreading in character. It is slow growing and "shrubby" in form.

CULTURE:

Light, semisunny. Temperature, 50° F (10° C) to 75° F (23° C). Humidity, 60% to 70%. Add extra peat moss and vermiculite to a standard potting soil, which should be allowed to partially dry between waterings. Good air circulation is very important. Needs a cool root system. Does not withstand people blight very well. Sensitive to chemicals of any kind (including pesticides). Subject to mealybugs, aphids, thrips, and red spiders.

DESIGN APPLICATION:

Specimen when young. Canopy (baffle in more mature plants).

SPECIES:

C. circinalis (Fern Palm), *C. revoluta* (Sago Palm).

4-26. *Cycas circinalis.*
(Courtesy, Tropical Ornamentals)

4-27. *Cycas revoluta.*
(Courtesy, Tropical Ornamentals)

NAME:

Cyperus (cy-per-us)

DESCRIPTION:

A semiaquatic member of the sedge family (Cyperaceae) from Madagascar. Reaches height of 4' to 6' (1.2 to 1.8 m). Its leaves form an "umbrella" shape and are attached to a long and narrow stem. The flowers are small and greenish in color, growing from the center of the "umbrella."

CULTURE:

Light, semisunny to semishady. Temperature, 55° F (12° C) to 80° F (26° C). Humidity, 40% to 50%. Add extra peat moss and perlite to a standard soil mix and keep it constantly moist, even soggy. Subject to mealybugs, whiteflies, mites, scale, and slugs. Do not use lime-based water.

DESIGN APPLICATION:

Baffle. Specimen in aquatic interiors.

SPECIES:

C. alternifolius, C. a. gracilis, C. a. variegatus, C. diffusus, C. papyrus.

NAME:

Dieffenbachia (diff-en-bac-ee-ah)

DESCRIPTION:

A member of the arum family (Araceae) from South America and the West Indies. Reaches height of 8′ (2.4 m). An attractive foliage plant for any interior landscape. The large green leaves are oblong and reach 18″ (45.7 cm). Some species are green with yellow, white, or gold patterns. The stems are thick and upright.

CULTURE:

Light, semisunny to shady. Temperature, 62° F (16° C) to 80° F (26° C). Humidity, 45% to 55%. Standard potting soil should be allowed to dry out between waterings. Subject to mealybugs, red spiders, scale, thrips, and aphids. Clean leaves often. Do not use leaf shiners.

DESIGN APPLICATION:

Accent specimen. Baffle.

SPECIES:

D. amoena, D. bausei, D. bowmanii, D. exotica, D. picta, D. seguina, D. splendens.

4-28. *Dieffenbachia amoena.*
(Courtesy, Tropical Ornamentals)

4-29. *Dieffenbachia Tropical Snow.*
(Courtesy, Tropical Ornamentals

NAME:

Dizygotheca (diz-ee-goth-ee-ca)

DESCRIPTION:

An evergreen member of the aralia family (Araliaceae) from the New Hebrides Islands in the Pacific. The slender, compound leaves (leaflets) are arranged on long and slender stems. Each leaf has a leathery texture, is dark green tinged with red color, and has a jagged edge. It may reach 10′ (3 m) in height.

CULTURE:

Light, semisunny to semishady. Temperature, 62° F (16° C) to 80° F (26° C). Humidity, 45% to 55%. Add extra peat moss and perlite to a standard soil mix, which should be allowed to dry out between waterings. Mist often. Subject to mealybugs, red spiders, scale, thrips, and aphids. Clean leaves often. Do not use leaf shiners.

DESIGN APPLICATION:

Baffle. Specimen in tub or accent planter.

SPECIES:

D. elegantissima, D. veitchii.

4-30. *Dizygotheca elegantissima.*

4-31. *Dizygotheca elegantissima.*

NAME:

Dracaena (dra-cee-na)

DESCRIPTION:

This member of the lily family (Liliaceae) is from tropical Africa. Reaches height of 20′ (6 m). Very decorative evergreen plants that comprise the most popular group for the interior landscape. Slow growing and adaptable to many situations. The leaves are narrow and sword shaped, from a central, erect stem. Multitrunks easily. A variety of foliage colors are available.

CULTURE:

Light, semisunny to shady. Temperature, 62° F (16° C) to 80° F (26° C). Humidity, 45% to 55%. Mist often. Standard soil mix should be allowed to dry out between waterings. Subject to mealybugs, red spiders, scale, thrips, and aphids. Clean leaves often.

DESIGN APPLICATION:

Specimen. Baffle. Masses for accent in larger planting areas.

SPECIES:

D. deremensis, D. d. Janet Craig, D. d. warneckii, D. draco (Dragon Tree), *D. fragrans* (Fragrant Dracaena), *D f. massangeana, D. godseffiana* (Gold Dust Dracaena), *D. goldieana, D. hookeriana, D. marginata* (Dragon Tree), *D. sanderiana* (Ribbon Plant), *D. s. Margret Berkery.*

4-32. *Dracaena deremensis Janet Craig.* (Courtesy, Tropical Ornamentals)

4-33. *Dracaena deremensis warneckii.*

4-34. *Dracaena draco.*

4-36. *Dracaena marginata.*
(Courtesy, Tropical Ornamentals)

4-35. *Dracaena fragrans massangeana.*
(Courtesy, Tropical Ornamentals)

4-37. *Dracaena sanderiana.*

NAME:

Episcia (ep-piss-e-ah)

DESCRIPTION:

A member of the gesneriad family (Gesneriaceae) from Columbia and Brazil. Reaches height of 2′ (.6 m). The leaves are bronzy, with distinct green or silver veining and grow to about 3″ (7.6 cm) long. Flowers are brilliant hues of pink, lavender, yellow, red, blue, and white.

CULTURE:

Light, semisunny to semishady. Temperature, 65° F (18° C) to 80° F (26° C). Humidity, 65% to 75%. Standard soil mix should have extra peat moss and extra sand and should be kept evenly moist. Mist often. Subject to nematodes, leaf miners, mealybugs, and mites, as well as root rot, crown rot, stem rot, and leaf spot (diseases caused by too much water). Avoid soggy soil.

DESIGN APPLICATION:

Groundcover mass. Accent mass.

SPECIES:

E. cupreata, E. dianthiflora, E. lilacina, E. punctata, E. reptans.

NAME:

Euphorbia (yer-for-be-ah)

DESCRIPTION:

This member of the spurge family (Euphorbiaceae) is from Mexico. Reaches to 4' (1.2 m) in height. The dark green leaves are lance shaped and lobed. The plant has a woody, shrublike character.

CULTURE:

Light, sunny to semisunny. Temperature, 50° F (10° C) to 75° F (23° C). Humidity, 40% to 50%. Standard soil mix should have extra vermiculite and one part sphagnum moss. Keep the soil evenly moist. Subject to red spiders, aphids, mealybugs, and scale. The leaves will drop from too much watering or a sharp temperature change.

DESIGN APPLICATION:

Accent mass (rotation only).

SPECIES:

E. drupifera, E. fulgens (scarlet), *E. pulcherrima* (Poinsettia).

NAME:

Fatshedera (fats-head-e-ra)

DESCRIPTION:

This tree ivy is a member of the ginseng family (Araliaceae) from France. Reaches 15′ (4.5 m) in length. The evergreen foliage is very interesting and can be applied as both a vine and a shrub. The leaves are dark green, glossy, and shaped like English Ivy.

CULTURE:

Light, sunny to semishady. Temperature, 62° F (16° C) to 80° F (26° C). Humidity, 45% to 55%. Mist often. Standard soil mix should be watered evenly. Subject to red spiders, scale, thrips, and aphids. Clean leaves often.

DESIGN APPLICATION:

Groundcover mass (trailing). Baffle (with structure).

SPECIES:

F. lizei (Ivy Tree), *F. l. variegata* (creamy white markings).

NAME:

Fatsia **(fat-see-ah)**

DESCRIPTION:

This member of the ginseng family (Araliaceae) is from Japan. Reaches 4' (1.2 m) in height. The evergreen foliage is attractive, shiny, lobed, and very wide. The flowers are small and whitish.

CULTURE:

Light, semisunny. Temperature, 50° F (10° C) to 80° F (26° C). Humidity, 45% to 55%. Standard soil mix should be watered thoroughly and evenly, allowing it to dry out between waterings. Subject to mealybugs, red spiders, scale, thrips, and aphids. Clean leaves often.

DESIGN APPLICATION:

Small shrub specimen. Baffle.

SPECIES:

F. japonica, F. j. moseri, F. j. variegata.

4-38. *Fatsia japonica.*
(Courtesy, Tropical Ornamentals)

NAME:

Ficus (fi-cus)

DESCRIPTION:

This dominant member of the fig family (Noraceae) is from the Mediterranean area. Depending upon the species, reaches up to 20′ (6 m) in height. A mixture of vines, shrubs, and small trees grown for the foliage and fruit. Many colors of leaves are available. A popular and durable evergreen group.

CULTURE:

Light, semisunny to shady. Temperature, 62° F (16° C) to 80° F (26° C). Humidity, 45% to 55%. Standard soil mix should be allowed to dry between thorough waterings. Multitrunks easily. Subject to mealybugs, red spiders, scale, thrips, and aphids. Clean leaves often.

DESIGN APPLICATION:

Very wide range, from groundcovers to canopies.

SPECIES:

F. benjamina (popular canopy), *F. diversifolia*, *F. elastica* (popular Rubber Plant), *F. e. 'Burgundy'*, *F. e. decora* (variegated Rubber Plant), *F. e. doescheri*, *F. lyrata*, *F. pandurata*, *F. pumila* (Creeping Fig), *F. radicans* (climber), *F. retusa*.

4-39. *Ficus benjamina.*

4-40. *Ficus elastica.*

4-41. *Ficus elastica.*

4-43. *Ficus elastica 'Burgundy.'*
(Courtesy, Tropical Ornamentals)

4-42. *Ficus elastica decora.*
(Courtesy, Tropical Ornamentals)

4-44. *Ficus pandurata.*

NAME:

Gardenia (gar-de-nia)

DESCRIPTION:

This member of the madder family (Rubiaceae) is from China. The plant reaches about 3′ (.9 m) in height. Tender evergreen shrubs grown mostly for their fragrant flowers. The foliage is very shiny, pointed, and dark green in color. The flowers are creamy white, about 2″ (5 cm) across.

CULTURE:

Light, sunny to semisunny. Temperature, 60° F (15° C) to 75° F (23° C). Humidity, 50% to 60%. Soil mix should be quite acid and should be kept evenly moist. Mist often. Subject to aphids, mealybugs, scale, and whiteflies. The tips of the leaves will turn black from the lack of water or when the temperature fluctuates too rapidly. When first planted, they may loose their buds or leaves due to planting shock (from the change in environment). Very difficult plant.

DESIGN APPLICATION:

Specimen in single container. Small shrub mass.

SPECIES:

G. jasminoides (Cape Jasmine), *G. stricta-nana*, *G. radicans*.

NAME:

Gynura (gye-nu-ra)

DESCRIPTION:

This member of the composite family (Compositae) is from Java. Reaches 3' (.9 m) in height. The velvet texture of the oval leaves with pointed tips creates an almost incandescent appearance. Both the leaves and stems are covered with a soft purple hair. The flowers are daisylike, orange or yellow.

CULTURE:

Light, sunny to semisunny. Temperature, 55° F (12° C) to 80° F (26° C). Humidity, 40% to 50%. Add extra peat moss and perlite to a standard soil mix; keep evenly moist. Mist often. Subject to mealybugs, whiteflies, mites, scale, and slugs. Do not overwater; it will rot easily.

DESIGN APPLICATION:

Groundcover mass. Accent mass.

SPECIES:

G. aurantiaca (Purple Velvet Plant), *G. sarmentosa* (Purple Passion Vine).

NAME:

Hedera (head-ah-ra)

DESCRIPTION:

A member of the ginseng family (Araliaceae) from North Africa, Europe, and Asia. The evergreen varieties are popular for interior landscapes and are adaptable to most situations. The leaves are usually lobed (three to five lobes); some have curled edges, some are pointed. The flowers are very small and not important.

4-45. *Hedera helix baltica.*

CULTURE:

Light, sunny to shady. Temperature, 55° F (12° C) to 80° F (26° C). Humidity, 40% to 50%. Add extra peat moss and perlite to a standard potting soil mix, and keep evenly moist. Mist often. Subject to mealybugs, mites, scale, and slugs. Clean foliage often.

DESIGN APPLICATION:

Groundcover mass. Hanging basket baffle.

SPECIES:

H. canariensis (Algerian Ivy), *H. c. variegata*, *H. helix* (English Ivy), *H. h. baltica* (Baltic Ivy), *H. h. fans*, *H. h. gold dust*, *H. h. hibernica*, *H. h. pedata*.

NAME:

Howeia (how-ee-ah)

DESCRIPTION:

These members of the palm family (Palmaceae) are from the Lord Howe islands in the Pacific. Reaches 15′ (4.5 m) in height. The foliage is long and arching; dark green in color. Erect growth habit; grows slowly, but needs lots of room at maturity.

CULTURE:

Light, semishady to shady. Temperature, 58° F (14° C) to 75° F (23° C). Humidity, 45% to 60%. Add extra peat moss to standard soil mix; water evenly. Mist often. Good air circulation is very important for proper growth. Subject to mealybugs, red spiders, and thrips. Avoid direct drafts. Clean foliage often. Multitrunks well.

DESIGN APPLICATION:

Baffle.

SPECIES:

H. belmoreana (Curley Palm), *H. fosteriana* (Paradise Palm).

NAME:

Hoya (hoy-ya)

DESCRIPTION:

A member of the milkweed family (Asclepiadaceae) from Java, East Asia, and Australia. Trailers reach 4' (1.2 m) in length. The leaves are oval, pointed, and somewhat fleshy. Twining habit, smooth-textured evergreen, with some species having showy colored leaves. Flowers are shiny and aromatic and come in a number of colors.

CULTURE:

Light, sunny or semisunny. Temperature, 60° F (15° C) to 75° F (23° C). Humidity, 30% to 40%. Add extra peat moss and perlite to a standard soil mix and allow it to dry between thorough waterings. Mist often. Subject to mites, mealybugs, nematodes, scale, and aphids. The roots will develop rot from too much watering.

DESIGN APPLICATION:

Specimen. Hanging basket baffle.

SPECIES:

H. australis, H. bella (Wax Plant), *H. carnosa, H. cinnamomifolia, H. coronaria, H. keysii, H. motoskei, H. purpureafusca.*

NAME:
Kalanchoe (cal-ank-oe)

DESCRIPTION:
A member of the stonecrop family (Crassulaceae) from South Africa, Asia, and Madagascar. Reaches several feet in height, shrublike or trailing. Succulent genus with flowers that are longlasting and attractive. The thick, succulent foliage, which is extremely interesting, can be linear, cylindrical, or ovate, depending on the species. The flowers are in clusters and are shaped like small stars. The blooms come in yellow, red, white, and rose.

CULTURE:
Light, sunny to semisunny. Temperature, 60° F (15° C) to 78° F (25° C). Humidity, 20% to 30%. Add extra perlite to a standard soil mix, allowing it to dry between even waterings. Mist lightly. Subject to mealybugs, aphids, mites, scale, and mildew (from too much humidity).

DESIGN APPLICATION:
Accent mass as groundcover.

SPECIES:
K. beharensis (arrow shaped leaves), *K. blossfeldiana* (Christmas Kalanchoe), *K. fedtschenkoi* (creeping habit), *K. lanceolata* (lance shaped leaves), *K. tomentosa* (Panda Plant), *K. uniflora* (bears one flower), *K. verticillata* (flowers in drooping clusters).

4-46. *Kalanchoe beharensis.*
(Courtesy, Tropical Ornamentals)

NAME:

Livistona (liv-is-toe-nah)

DESCRIPTION:

This member of the palm family (Palmaceae) is from Eastern Asia. Reaches 10′ (3 m) in height. The foliage often reaches 5′ (1.5 m) in width, growing from a single stem, opening in semicircles as open fans. The arching stems are attached to a single trunk. Slow growing.

CULTURE:

Light, semishady to shady. Temperature, 58° F (14° C) to 75° F (23° C). Humidity, 45% to 60%. Good air circulation is very important. Standard soil mix should have extra peat moss and vermiculite, and should be allowed to dry between thorough waterings. Subject to mealybugs, red spiders, scale, and thrips. Clean foliage often.

DESIGN APPLICATION:

Baffle for smaller plants. Canopy for older, larger plants. Specimen.

SPECIES:

L. australis (Australian Fan Palm), *L. chinensis* (Chinese Fan Palm).

NAME:

Maranta (mar-an-ta)

DESCRIPTION:

This member of the arrowroot family (Marantaceae) is from South America. Reaches 3' (.9 m) in height. A very durable and attractive group with colorful foliage. The oval shaped, gray green leaves with deep green shades are sometimes purple underneath and red-veined throughout. The white to pink flowers will bloom if the culture is right.

4-47. *Maranta sp.*

CULTURE:

Light, semishady to semisunny. Temperature, 62° F (16° C) to 80° F (26° C). Humidity, 45% to 55%. Standard potting soil should have extra peat moss and perlite. Allow soil to dry between waterings. Subject to mealybugs, red spiders, scale, thrips, and aphids. Clean foliage often. Avoid leaf shiners.

DESIGN APPLICATION:

Groundcover mass.

SPECIES:

(all referred to as Prayer Plant)
M. arundinacea (bamboo-like), *M. a. variegata* (cream-edged leaves), *M. bicolor* (two-colored leaves), *M. Kerchoviana* (pale gray leaves), *M. massangeana* (gray green leaves).

NAME:

Monstera (mon-ster-a)

DESCRIPTION:

This member of the arum family (Araceae) is from Mexico and Guatemala. Grows rapidly to 10′ (3 m) or more. One of the most durable of all groups for the interior landscape. Often called the Split-leaf Philodendron, it is actually a vine. The leaves are dark green, broad, and lobed (resembles Swiss cheese). The flowers are creamy white and will bloom easily. The cone shaped fruit is edible when it matures.

CULTURE:

Light, semisunny to shady. Temperature, 62° F (16° C) to 80° F (26° C). Humidity, 45% to 55%. Standard potting soil should be allowed to dry out between waterings. Subject to mealybugs, red spiders, scale, thrips, and aphids. Clean leaves often.

DESIGN APPLICATION:

Baffle.

SPECIES:

M. acuminata (pointed leaves), *M. deliciosa* (Split-leaf Philodendron), *M. dubia*, *M. pertusa* (small leaves, vigorous).

4-48. *Monstera deliciosa.*

NAME:

Nephrolepis (nef-rol-ep-is)

DESCRIPTION:

This member of the fern family (Polypodiaceae) is from tropical America. The leaves (fronds) arise directly from the soil surface to about 5' (1.5 m) in length. A rapidly growing evergreen group, with excellent all-around characteristics for the interior landscape.

4-49. *Nephrolepis exaltata bostoniensis.*

CULTURE:

Light, semisunny to semishady. Temperature, 50° F (10° C) to 75° F (23° C). Humidity, 60% to 70%. Add extra peat moss and vermiculite to a standard soil mix, which should partially dry between waterings. Subject to mealybugs, aphids, and red spiders. Needs cool roots. Be careful with pesticides.

DESIGN APPLICATION:

Shrub mass as barrier.

4-50. *Nephrolepis e. b. Fluffy Ruffle.*

SPECIES:

N. acuminata, N. biserrata, N. cordifolia, N. exaltata bostoniensis (Boston Fern), *N. e. b. childsii* (dwarf), *N. e. b. Fluffy Ruffle* (Fluffy Ruffle Fern), *N. e. b. norwoodii* (lacelike fronds), *N. e. b. verona* (Boston Fern), *N. pectinata* (Basket Fern).

NAME:

Pandanus (pan-day-nus)

DESCRIPTION:

A member of the screw pine family (Pandanaceae) from Polynesia. Reaches to 10′ (3 m) in height. A decorative group that resembles a palm tree without a trunk. The sword shaped leaves are long and have prickly margins. Rarely flowers in cultivation.

CULTURE:

Light, sunny to semisunny. Temperature, 62° F (16° C) to 80° F (26° C). Humidity, 45% to 55%. Standard soil mix should be allowed to dry out between waterings. Subject to mealybugs, red spiders, scale, thrips, and aphids. Clean foliage often. Use leaf shiners carefully.

DESIGN APPLICATION:

Baffle. Shrub mass.

SPECIES:

P. baptistii (blue green and yellow leaves), *P. sanderi* (yellow green striped), *P. utilis* (bluish green leaves), *P. veitchii* (Screw Pine), *P. v. compacta.*

4-51. *Pandanus utilis.*
(Courtesy, Tropical Ornamentals)

NAME:

Peperomia (pep-per-rome-ee-ah)

DESCRIPTION:

A member of the pepper family (Piperaceae) from South America. Reaches height of 18″ (45.7 cm). A succulentlike plant with fleshy, smooth-edged leaves in numerous colors and variations. Small-scale material, with small leaves containing striations, variegations, blotches, and spots. Growth habits range from erect to creeping (depending upon species). Flowers are usually insignificant.

4-52. *Peperomia argyreia.*
(Courtesy, Tropical Ornamentals)

CULTURE:

Light, semisunny to shady. Temperature, 55° F (12° C) to 80° F (26° C). Humidity, 40% to 50%. Standard soil should have extra peat moss and perlite and should be allowed to become dry between waterings. Subject to mealybugs, whiteflies, mites, and slugs. Will rot easily from overwatering. Clean foliage often.

DESIGN APPLICATION:

Groundcover, accent mass.

SPECIES:

P. acuminata (grasslike, prickly), *P. argyreia* (Watermelon Peperomia), *P. bicolor* (grayish green, silver edges), *P. caperata* (wrinkle-leafed), *P. clusiifolia* (metallic green), *P. crassifolia* (thick leaved), *P. glabella*, *P. g. variegata* (light green and yellow), *P. griseoargentea* (Ivy Peperomia), *P. incana* (heart shaped leaves), *P. maculosa* (spotted leaves), *P. marmorata* (mottled leaves), *P. metallica* (waxy leaves, brown), *P. obtusifolia* (Blunt-leaf Peperomia), *P. o. alba* (white leaves), *P. o. variegata* (pale green with white edges), *P. ornata*, *P. rotundifolia* (rounded leaves), *P. velutina* (Velvet Peperomia).

NAME:

Philodendron (phil-o-den-dron)

DESCRIPTION:

This member of the arum family (Araceae) is from Central and South America. Reaches 7' to 8' (2.1 to 2.4 m) in height. A very well-known and adaptable material to almost any interior landscape, it has a glossy green foliage in various patterns and shapes. Some are climbers, some are shrubs, others are erect in habit.

CULTURE:

Light, semisunny to shady. Temperature, 62° F (16° C) to 80° F (26° C). Humidity, 45% to 55%. Standard potting soil should be watered thoroughly, but allowed to dry before watering again. Subject to mealybugs, red spiders, scale, thrips, aphids, and brown spots (from overwatering). Becomes spindly in too little light. Clean leaves often. Avoid drafts.

DESIGN APPLICATION:

Specimen to baffle (varies with species).

SPECIES:

Solid-leaved climbers: *P. amurense*, *P. andreanum* (Black Gold), *P. hastatum* (arrow shaped leaves), *P. micans*, *P. oxycardium* (silky iridescent leaves), *P. sodiroi* (heart-shaped leaves), *P. verrucosum* (velvety leaves). Cut-leaved climbers: *P. panduraeforme*, *P. pertusum*, *P. radiatum*, *P. squamiferum* (deeply lobed). Solid-leaved, self-heading: *P. cannifolium* (sword shaped), *P. undulatum* (arrow shaped), *P. wendlandii* (long, oval shaped). Cut-leaved, self-heading: *P. bipinnatifidum* (large cuts in leaf), *P. selloum* (deeply lobed).

4-53. *Philodendron Angel Wing.*
(Courtesy, Tropical Ornamentals)

4-54. *Philodendron selloum.*

NAME:

Phoenix (phee-nix)

DESCRIPTION:

This member of the palm family (Palmaceae) is from Africa and Asia. It is a slow-growing, attractive material that withstands abuse. Ranges in colors from green to blue green. The leaves (fronds) reach several feet in length; they grow from a single stem and have an arching habit.

CULTURE:

Light, semishady to semisunny. Temperature, 58° F (14° C) to 75° F (23° C). Humidity, 45% to 60%. Standard soil mix should have extra peat moss and vermiculite. Allow the soil to dry out between waterings. Subject to mealybugs, red spiders, scale, and thrips. Clean leaves often. No direct sun. Good air circulation is important.

DESIGN APPLICATION:

Baffle.

SPECIES:

P. canariensis (feathery fronds), *P. dactylifera* (Date Palm), *P. roebelenii* (Pygmy Date Palm).

NAME:

Pilea (pi-lee-ah)

DESCRIPTION:

A member of the nettle family (Urticaceae) from Indochina and tropical America. Reaches 2' (.6 m) in height. The oval leaves are fleshy in character and deeply veined or crinkled. Some are hairy in nature. Growing habit ranges from erect to creeping. Mostly green with variations of blue green, blue silver, purple, and copper.

CULTURE:

Light, semisunny to semishady. Temperature, 55° F (12° C) to 80° F (26° C). Humidity, 40% to 50%. Standard soil should have extra peat moss and perlite and should be kept evenly moist. Subject to mealybugs, scale, and slugs. Clean leaves often. Do not allow soil to dry out.

DESIGN APPLICATION:

Groundcover. Accent mass.

SPECIES:

P. cadierei (Aluminum Plant), *P. depressa*, *P. involucrata*, *P. microphylla*, *P. moon valley*, *P. nummularifolia*, *P. pubescens*, *P. repens*.

NAME:

Platycerium (plat-ty-seer-ee-um)

DESCRIPTION:

This member of the fern family (Polypodiaceae) is from Australia. Reaches several feet in height. In natural habitat grows primarily on other plants (trunks). Leaves (fronds) are either disc shaped (sterile fronds) and bright green in color, or erect and lobed (fertile fronds) and grayish green in color with deep veins.

CULTURE:

Light, semisunny to semishady. Temperature, 55° F (12° C) to 80° F (26° C). Humidity, 60% to 70%. Good air circulation is very important, but avoid drafts. Use sphagnum moss in specially prepared packages. Do not use potting soil. Water and mist often, but do not soak fertile fronds. Subject to mealybugs, aphids, thrips, and red spiders.

DESIGN APPLICATION:

Accent specimen.

SPECIES:

P. bifurcatum, P. b. majus, P. grande, P. hillii, P. pumilum, P. stemaria, P. veitchii, P. wilhelminae-reginae.

NAME:

Podocarpus (po-do-car-pus)

DESCRIPTION:

A member of the podocarpus family (Podocarpaceae) from China and Japan. Can reach 10′ (3 m) in height. An evergreen material that gives a "pine needle" effect. The foliage is dense, bright green when young, dark green when older. One of the newer members for the interior landscape.

4-55. *Podocarpus macrophyllus maki.*

CULTURE:

Light, semisunny to semishady. Temperature, 40° F (4° C) to 80° F (26° C). Humidity, 30% to 40%. Standard soil mix should have extra sand so it can dry thoroughly before watering. Mist often. Good air circulation is important. Subject to aphids, mealybugs, mites, scale, and leaf miners.

DESIGN APPLICATION:

Screen.

SPECIES:

P. macrophyllus maki (Japanese Yew), *P. nagi.*

NAME:

Polyscias (pol-is-ee-us)

DESCRIPTION:

This member of the aralia family (Araliaceae) is from many of the Pacific islands, Africa, and Asia. May reach 10' (3 m) in height. The leaves are compound and are found in shades of green with creamy accents. The small shrublike appearance with "ferny" leaves makes it a very attractive material.

CULTURE:

Light, sunny to shady. Temperature, 62° F (16° C) to 80° F (26° C). Humidity, 50% to 60%. Standard soil mix should be allowed to dry between waterings. Mist often. Subject to mealybugs, red spiders, scale, thrips, and aphids. Clean leaves often.

DESIGN APPLICATION:

Baffle.

SPECIES:

P. balfouriana (Balfour Aralia), *P. b. marginata, P. fruticosa, P. guilfoylei, P. g. victoriae* (Victoria Aralia).

NAME:

Ruellia (rew-ell-ee-ah)

DESCRIPTION:

This member of the acanthus family (Acanthaceae) is from Brazil. Has a bushy habit that may reach 4' (1.2 m) in height. Grown for both foliage and flowers. The leaves are oval in shape and variegated, and they have a velvety texture. The flowers are bell shaped and colored white to pink or purple to crimson.

CULTURE:

Light, semisunny to semishady. Temperature, 55° F (12° C) to 75° F (23° C). Humidity, 60% to 70%. Add extra sand to standard soil mix and keep it evenly moist. Mist often. Subject to red spiders and thrips. Too little humidity or direct sun will cause leaves to roll up.

DESIGN APPLICATION:

Small shrub mass.

SPECIES:

R. amoena (crimson flowers, climbing), *R. devosiana* (Christmas Pride), *R. macrantha* (large flowers), *R. makoyane* (olive green foliage).

NAME:

Sansevieria (san-sa-ver-ee-ah)

DESCRIPTION:

A member of the lily family (Liliaceae) from Africa and India. A hardy group that will withstand adverse conditions. The leaves are thick, upright, and sword shaped. Reach up to 3' (.9 m) in length. They are green with pale green stripes and horizontal zigzags.

CULTURE:

Light, sunny to shady (tolerant to many extremes). Temperature, 62° F (16° C) to 80° F (26° C). Humidity, 25% to 35%. Standard soil mix should be allowed to dry between waterings.

DESIGN APPLICATION:

Accent specimen.

SPECIES:

S. cylindrica (spearlike leaves), *S. ehrenbergii*, *S. parva* (concave leaves), *S. thyrsiflora* (Snake Plant, long, narrow leaves), *S. trifasciata*, *S. t. golden hahnii* (gray green leaves), *S. t. laurentii* (broad yellow edges), *S. t. silver Hahnii* (silver green leaves), *S. zeylanica* (leaves in rosettes).

4-56. *Sansevieria trifasciata.*

4-57. *Sansevieria cylindrica.*
(Courtesy, Tropical Ornamentals)

NAME:

Schefflera (schef-e-ler-ah)
See *Brassaia*

NAME:

Scindapsus (cin-dap-sus)

DESCRIPTION:

This member of the arum family (Araceae) is from the East Indies. A very popular and widely used ivy. Its leaves are waxy, green and yellow striped. The tiny flowers seldom bloom in the interior landscape. Often called Pothos Ivy, but it is not a true *Pothos*.

CULTURE:

Light, semisunny to semishady. Temperature, 62° F (16° C) to 80° F (26° C). Humidity, 45% to 55%. Standard soil mix should be allowed to dry between waterings. Mist often. Clean leaves often. Higher light qualities increase leaf color.

DESIGN APPLICATION:

Baffle in hanging baskets. Groundcover.

SPECIES:

S. aureus (Devil's Ivy), *S. a. marble queen*, *S. a. tricolor*, *S. pictus*, *S. p. argyraeus* (Silver Pothos).

4-58. *Schefflera actinophylla.*

4-59. *Scindapsus aureus.*
(Courtesy, Tropical Ornamentals)

NAME:

Sedum (see-dome)

DESCRIPTION:

This member of the stonecrop family (Crassulaceae) is from central Mexico to Peru. It has a low, spreading habit of growth. The thick, fleshy leaves overlap to form brades or pendants. Flowers are pale pink to red.

CULTURE:

Light, sunny to semisunny. Temperature, 50° F (10° C) to 80° F (26° C). Humidity, 20% to 25%. Standard soil needs extra sand, so it can become quite dry between waterings. Subject to scale, mealybugs, and root rot from overwatering. Very delicate; avoid people blight.

DESIGN APPLICATION:

Groundcover.

SPECIES:

(There are numerous species of *Sedum*. The following are more applicable to the interior landscape.) *S. adolphi* (Golden Sedum), *S. allantoides*, *S. dasyphyllum* (creeping habits), *S. lineare*, *S. morganianum* (Donkey's Tail), *S. multiceps*, *S. praealtum*, *S. rubrotinctum*, *S. sieboldii*, *S. s. medio-variegatum*, *S. stahlii* (Coral Beads).

4-60. *Sedum sp.*

NAME:

Setcreasea (set-creas-ee-ah)

DESCRIPTION:

This member of the spiderwort family (Commelinaceae) is from Mexico. Reaches 3′ (.9 m) in height. A very strong purple foliage color and a pendulous habit of growth make this material very popular. The leaves are lance shaped, hairy, long, and tender. The pink to lilac flowers are small and bloom on the tips of the stems.

4-61. *Setcreasea purpurea.*

CULTURE:

Light, sunny to semisunny. Temperature, 55° F (12° C) to 80° F (26° C). Humidity, 40% to 50%. Add extra peat moss and perlite to a standard soil mix, and keep it evenly moist. Mist daily. Subject to mealybugs, whiteflies, mites, scale, and slugs. It will rot easily when overwatered. Clean foliage often.

DESIGN APPLICATION:

Groundcover. Accent mass. Baffle from a hanging basket.

SPECIES:

S. purpurea (Purple Heart).

4-62. *Spathiphyllum sp.*

NAME:

Spathiphyllum (spath-e-phy-lum)

DESCRIPTION:

A member of the arum family (Araceae) from Central and South America. Reaches 3′ (.9 m) in height. This popular evergreen has shiny, dark, evergreen, lance-shaped leaves. The flowers are on a long spike and are of a white spathe surrounding a small yellow spadix.

CULTURE:

Light, semisunny to shady. Temperature, 65° F (18° C) to 85° F (29° C). Humidity, 70% to 80%. Add extra peat moss to a standard soil mix, and keep evenly moist. Mist often. Subject to red spiders, mealybugs, whiteflies, and scale. Clean leaves often.

DESIGN APPLICATION:

Medium shrub mass.

SPECIES:

S. cannifolium, S. clevelandii, S. floribundum.

NAME:

Tradescantia (trad-es-cant-ee-ah)

DESCRIPTION:

This member of the spiderwort family (Commelinaceae) is from Central and South America. Its vining habit makes this material very popular for the interior landscape. The leaves are basically green and oval in shape and are accented in violet and silver with violet undersides. The stems are reddish. Flowers are very small and grow at the end of the stem.

4-63. *Tradescantia albiflora albo-vittata.*

CULTURE:

Light, sunny to semishady. Temperature, 55° F (12° C) to 80° F (26° C). Humidity, 40% to 50%. Standard soil mix needs extra perlite and should be kept evenly moist. Mist often. Subject to mealybugs, whiteflies, mites, scale, and slugs. Prune plant often. It will rot easily from overwatering. Clean leaves often.

DESIGN APPLICATION:

Groundcover.

SPECIES:

T. albiflora (green leaves, white flowers), *T. a. albo-vittata*, *T. a. laekenensis* (Rainbow Tuck Plant), *T. blossfeldiana*, *T. b. variegata*, *T. fluminensis* (Wandering Jew), *T. f. variegata* (variegated Wandering Jew), *T. multiflora* (many flowers, *T. navicularis*.

NAME:

Zebrina (zee-bri-na) See *Tradescantia fluminensis*

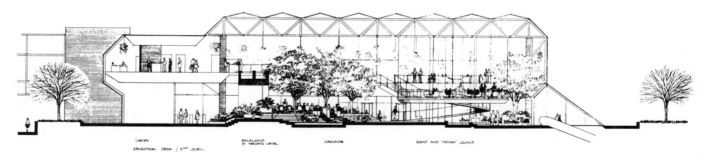

CHOPS
RECEPTION DESK / 2ND LEVEL   ESCALATOR TO SECOND LEVEL   CASCADE   RAMP AND 'MIDWAY' LOUNGE

HYATT REGENCY CHICAGO ADDITION
PRELIMINARY LANDSCAPE PLAN
CROSS SECTION A-A.
LAND DESIGN RESEARCH, INC.   AUGUST 30, 1977
SCALE 1/8"=1'-0"

A-1 This section of the Hyatt Regency Planting Plan illustrates the different visual experiences the interior planting has created for the hotel guests. (*Courtesy, Land/Design Research, Inc.*)

Appendix A
PLANTING PLAN GRAPHICS

The Components of the Planting Plan

The sheet layout for the interior planting plans is important and should be well composed. The plan contains a large amount of information, and the arrangement of all the plan components should be taken into careful consideration. The following outline contains the necessary components to be located on the plan. It should be noted that this list will vary according to the size of the project and the scale of the drawing. For example, in order to obtain a manageable scale on large projects, more than one drawing may be necessary. However, only one plant schedule should be necessary for each project. The elements to be included are as follows:

A. scale, both written and graphic

B. north orientation

C. existing planters (stationary)

D. interior structures (walls), overhangs

E. details as needed (a separate sheet is usually required)

F. title block
1. name of project
2. address of project
3. designer
    a. name
    b. address of firm
4. name or initials of drafter
5. date
6. page number

G. plant schedule
1. item number (or symbol used)
2. number of plants (totals)
3. plant name (common and botanical)
4. size and condition of plant
    a. size
        (1) container
        (2) height desired
        (3) caliper of tree
    b. condition
        (1) size of container
        (2) balled and burlapped (B&B)
        (3) bare root (B.R.)
        (4) spacing
5. notes where required, such as "multitrunk"
6. cost estimate

Some representative samples of interior-planting graphics are also shown.

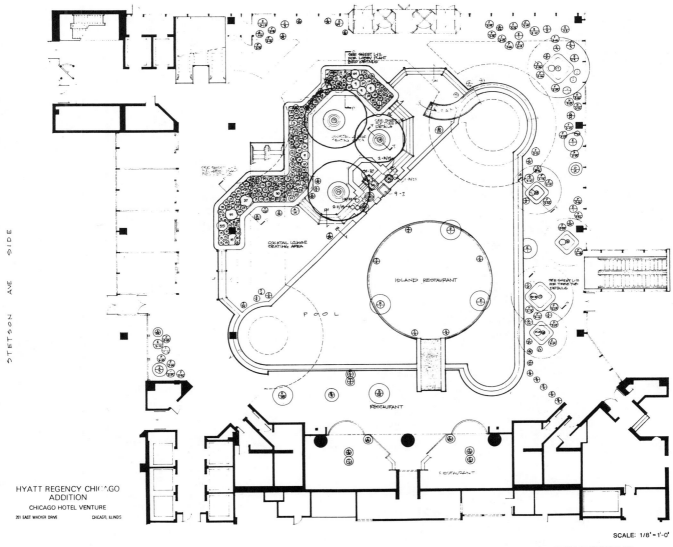

SCALE: 1/8" = 1'-0'

PLAZA LEVEL-INTERIOR PLANTING PLAN

A-2 The final planting plan uses a key to specify the location for each plant. At this scale, the key is the most practical method for specifying plant materials. (*Courtesy, Land/Design Research, Inc.*)

I. INTERIOR LANDSCAPING—PLAN
A. *Plant Material*

Code	Quantity	Item
1	11	*Kentia fosteriana* 7-8′ ht.; multitrunks; 10 gal.
36	10	**Kentia fosteriana* 4-5′ ht.; multitrunks; 7 gal.
2	3	*Brassaia actinophylla* Schefflera 12-14′ ht.; multistemmed full heads; 40 gal.
3	11	**Brassaia actinophylla* Schefflera 6-8′ ht.; multistemmed full heads; 15 gal.
4	33	*Brassaia actinophylla* Schefflera 4-5′ ht.; multistemmed full heads; 7 gal.
5	6	*Chamaedora erumpens* Bamboo Palm 6-7′ ht.; multistemmed; 10 gal.
37	3	*Chamaedora erumpens* Bamboo Palm 4-5′ ht.; multistemmed; 7 gal.
6	29	*Chlorophytum vittatum* Spider Plant 10″ pots with 5-6 flyers per plant
7	33	*Cissus rhombifolia (Vitis)* Grape Ivy 10″ pots
33	1	*Clusia rosea* Tree Form 4-5′ ht.; 6′ spread
9	25	**Codiaeum Croton 'America'* American Croton 3-4′ ht.
10	72	*Codiaeum Croton 'America'* American Croton 2-3′ ht.
12	14	*Diffenbachia amonea* 6″ pots; 18-24″ spread
13		*Dracaena deremensis 'Janet Craig'* Dracaene Janet Craig
	18	18-24″ spread; 3 pots per planter (use in fiberglass planters)
	80	15-18″ spread; 2 pots per planter (use as ground cover)
14	3	*Dracaena marginata* 6-8′ ht.; multistemmed heavy specimen; 15 gal.
15		*Dracaena warneckei* Daracaena Warneck
	37	18-24″ spread; 3 pots per planter (use in fiberglass planters)
	54	15-18″ spread; 2 pots per planter (use as ground cover)
16	4	*Dracaena warneckei* Dracaene Warneck 3-4′ height; 12″ pot
17	4	*Ficus nitida benjamina* Ficus tree 8-10″ cal.; 20-24′ ht.; 18-20′ spread, 200 gal.; single or multistemmed to be field selected
18	4	*Ficus nitida benjamina* Ficus tree 5-6″ cal.; 16-18′ ht.; 14-16′ spread; 95 gal.; single or multistemmed to be field selected
19	1	*Ficus nitida benjamina* Ficus tree 3 1/2-4″ cal.; 10-12′ ht.; 8-10′ spread, single stem
20	267	*Ficus pumila repens* Creeping Fig 2 1/2-3′ pots
22	49	**Nephrolepis exaltata* Boston Fern 18-24″ spread; 8″ pot
23	3	*Phoenix roebelenii* Pygmy Palm 5-6′ spread
24	16	**Phoenix roebelenii* Pygmy Palm 2-3′ spread

25	12	*Philodendron oxycardium* Cordatum Philodendron 10″ pots; 1 plant per planter; 15-18″ runners
26	7	*Philodendron Selloum* Selloum Philodendron 3-4′ spread; 12″ pot
27	5	*Philodendron Selloum* Selloum Philodendron 2-3′ spread; 12″ pot
34	2	*Pittosporum tobira* 3-3 1/2′ spread (selected low plants)
28	7	*Raphis excelsa* Lady Palm 5-6′ ht.
35	2	*Raphis excelsa* Lady Palm 2-3′ ht.
29		*Spathiphyllum "mauna loa"* White Flag Plant
	40	24-30″ spread; 10″ pots (use in fiberglass planters)
	86	24-30″ spread; 6″ pots (use as ground cover)
30	7	*Spathiphyllum "mauna loa"* White Flag Plant 3-4′ spread
32	140	*Flowers, 6 1/2″ pots, 5 pots per planter

B. *Planters*

L	83	*Wicker Hanging Planters includes 14 ft. of 1/2″ link black chain, clamps, and/or hooks/planter Fiberglass Planters Smooth finish/dark brown (Greco Bronze) Leaf Fiberglass 4865 N.W. 37th Ave. Miami, FLA or approved equal
B	4	48″ dia. × 27″ ht.
E	18	30″ dia. × 25″ ht.
F	43	30″ dia. × 16″ ht.
G	36	*24″ dia. × 21″ ht.
H	6	24″ dia. × 16″ ht.
I	59	*20″ dia. × 20″ ht.
J	9	20″ dia. × 16″ ht.

K	65	12″ dia. × 16″ ht.

C. *Soil/Gravel, etc.*

3,900 CF	Plant Mix (W.R. Grace Metro-Mix)
2,050 SF	Fiberglass blanket or spun polypropylene
660 CF	Gravel
3,500 SF	4 mil polyethylene vapor barrier
72	Polyethylene bags for hanging planters
72	Sphagnum moss for hanging planters

NOTE: Plants and planters marked with asterisk (*) are not all located on the plans. The following items are to be used as infill where needed during installation. (These items are already included in the above list):

3	*Kentia fosteriana*, 4-5′ ht. in G planters (3)
3	*Brassaia actinophylla*, 6-8′, ht. in I planters (3)
8	*Codiaeum Croton*, 3-4′ ht. in G planters (8)
8	*Codiaeum Croton*, 3-4′ ht. without planters
3	*Nephrolepis exalta* in hanging planters (3)
3	*Phoenix roebelenii*, 2-3′ spd. in I planters (3)
2	*Raphis excelsa*, 5-6′ ht. without planters
20	*Spathiphyllum*, 6″ pots, use as ground cover
50	Flowers 6 1/2″ pots, without planters

Soil, gravel, etc. are included in above list.

II. INTERIOR LANDSCAPING—Areas other than lobby, reception level, bridge, and existing hotel

Quantity	Item
40	*Brassaia actinophylla* Schefflera 4-5′ ht.; multistemmed full heads; 7 gal.
60	*Dracaena warneckei* Dracaena Warneck 3-4′ ht.; 12″ pot
200	*Spathiphyllum "mauna loa"* White Flag Plant 24-30″ spread
380 CF	Plant Mix (W.R. Grace Metro-Mix)
380 SF	Fiberglass blanket
95 CF	Gravel
200	12″ dia. × 16″ ft. Fiberglass planter dark brown
100	20″ dia. × 16″ ht. Fiberglass planter dark brown

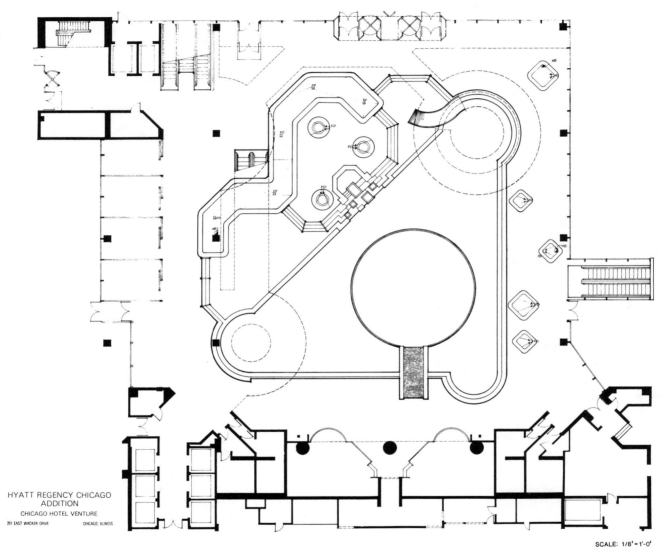

SCALE: 1/8" = 1'-0"

PLAZA LEVEL-INTERIOR DRAINAGE PLAN

HYATT REGENCY CHICAGO
ADDITION
CHICAGO HOTEL VENTURE
201 EAST WACKER DRIVE   CHICAGO, ILLINOIS

LD
R   **LAND DESIGN / RESEARCH, INC.**
ONE MALL NORTH   SUITE 400
COLUMBIA, MARYLAND

A-3 The Plaza Level Drainage Plan illustrates the necessity for
control of water from the interior planters. (*Courtesy, Land/
Design Research, Inc.*)

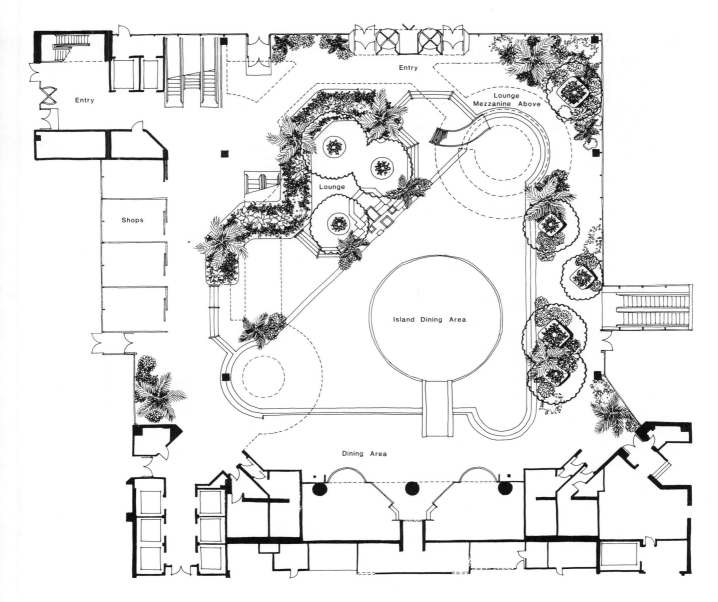

A-4 The final planting plan can be illustrated by using the symbolic graphic technique for improved client communication. (*Courtesy, Land/Design Research, Inc.*)

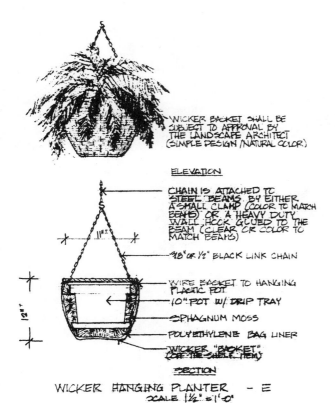

WICKER BASKET SHALL BE SUBJECT TO APPROVAL BY THE LANDSCAPE ARCHITECT (SIMPLE DESIGN /NATURAL COLOR)

ELEVATION

CHAIN IS ATTACHED TO STEEL BEAMS BY EITHER A SMALL CLAMP (COLOR TO MATCH BEAM) OR A HEAVY DUTY WALL HOOK GLUED TO THE BEAM (CLEAR OR COLOR TO MATCH BEAMS)

3/8" OR 1/2" BLACK LINK CHAIN

WIRE BASKET TO HANGING PLASTIC POT

10" POT W/ DRIP TRAY

SPHAGNUM MOSS

POLYETHYLENE BAG LINER

WICKER "BASKET" (OFF THE SHELF ITEM)

SECTION

WICKER HANGING PLANTER - E
SCALE 1½" = 1'-0"

A-5 Decorative liners can be used for planter pots to provide a variety of interior accents. (*Courtesy, Land/ Design Research, Inc.*)

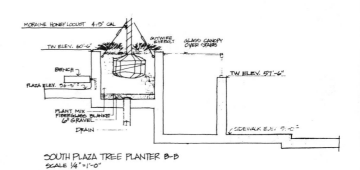

MORAINE HONEY LOCUST 4-5" CAL.
TW. ELEV. 60'-6"
GUY WIRE EYE BOLT
GLASS CANOPY OVER STAIRS
BENCH
PLAZA ELEV. 56'-3"
TW. ELEV. 57'-6"
PLANT MIX
FIBERGLASS BLANKET
6" GRAVEL
DRAIN
SIDEWALK ELEV. 51'-0"

SOUTH PLAZA TREE PLANTER B-B
SCALE ¼"=1'-0"

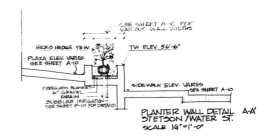

SEE SHEET A-10 FOR VARIOUS WALL WIDTHS
HICKS HEDGE YEW
TW. ELEV. 56'-6"
PLAZA ELEV. VARIES SEE SHEET A-10
FIBERGLASS BLANKET
6" GRAVEL
DRAIN
BUBBLER IRRIGATION— SEE SHEET P-10 FOR DETAILS
SIDEWALK ELEV. VARIES SEE SHEET A-10

PLANTER WALL DETAIL A-A'
STETSON /WATER ST.
SCALE ¼"=1'-0"

A-6 Sections of the various planter walls illustrate the relationships to walks and seating areas. (*Courtesy, Land/Design Research, Inc.*)

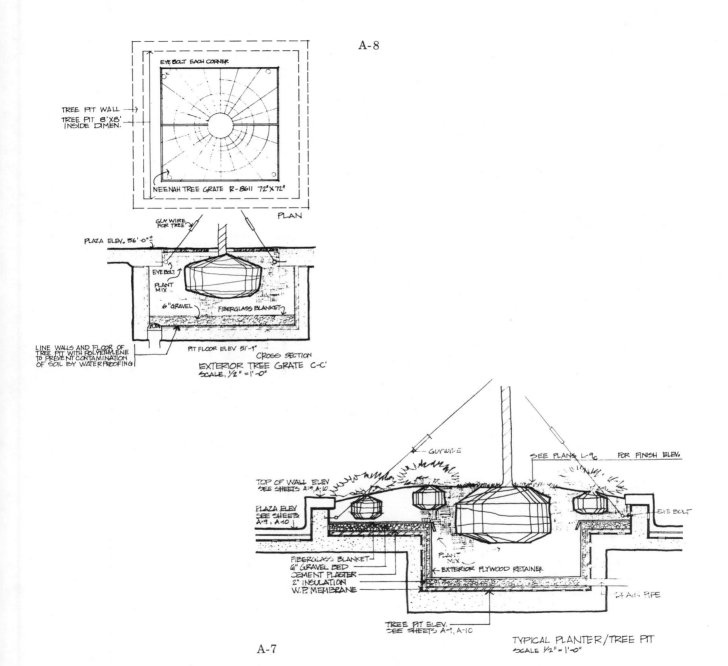

A-8

EYE BOLT EACH CORNER

TREE PIT WALL

TREE PIT 8'X8' INSIDE DIMEN.

NEENAH TREE GRATE R-8611 72"X72"

PLAN

GUY WIRE FOR TREE

PLAZA ELEV. 56'-0"±

EYE BOLT

PLANT MIX

6" GRAVEL

FIBERGLASS BLANKET

LINE WALLS AND FLOOR OF TREE PIT WITH POLYETHYLENE TO PREVENT CONTAMINATION OF SOIL BY WATERPROOFING

PIT FLOOR ELEV 51'-9"

CROSS SECTION
EXTERIOR TREE GRATE C-C'
SCALE, 1/2" = 1'-0"

GUY WIRE

SEE PLANS L-9₆ FOR FINISH ELEV.

TOP OF WALL ELEV SEE SHEETS A-9, A-10

PLAZA ELEV SEE SHEETS A-9, A-10

EYE BOLT

FIBERGLASS BLANKET
6" GRAVEL BED
CEMENT PLASTER
2" INSULATION
W.P. MEMBRANE

PLANT MIX

EXTERIOR PLYWOOD RETAINER

DRAIN PIPE

TREE PIT ELEV. SEE SHEETS A-9, A-10

A-7

TYPICAL PLANTER/TREE PIT
SCALE 1/2" = 1'-0"

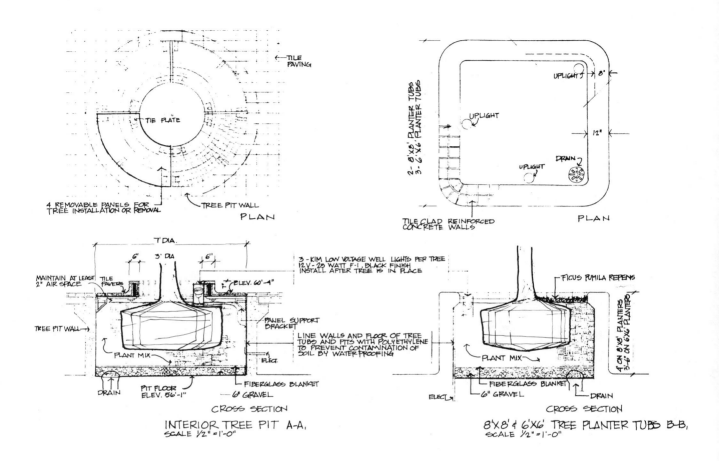

TILE
PAVING

TILE PLATE

4 REMOVABLE PANELS FOR
TREE INSTALLATION OR REMOVAL

TREE PIT WALL

P L A N

2 - 8'X8' PLANTER TUBS
3 - 6'X6' PLANTER TUBS

UPLIGHT

UPLIGHT

8"

12"

UPLIGHT

DRAIN

TILE CLAD REINFORCED
CONCRETE WALLS

P L A N

7' DIA.

6"   3' DIA.   6"

MAINTAIN AT LEAST
2" AIR SPACE

TILE
PAVERS

ELEV. 60'-4"

3 - KIM LOW VOLTAGE WELL LIGHTS PER TREE
12 V - 25 WATT F-I, BLACK FINISH
INSTALL AFTER TREE IS IN PLACE

TREE PIT WALL

PANEL SUPPORT
BRACKET

LINE WALLS AND FLOOR OF TREE
TUBS AND PITS WITH POLYETHYLENE
TO PREVENT CONTAMINATION OF
SOIL BY WATER PROOFING

FICUS PUMILA REPENS

PLANT MIX

ELECT.

PLANT MIX

4 ON 8'X8' PLANTERS
3-6" ON 6'X6' PLANTERS

DRAIN

PIT FLOOR
ELEV. 56'-1"

FIBERGLASS BLANKET

6" GRAVEL

ELECT.

FIBERGLASS BLANKET

6" GRAVEL

DRAIN

CROSS SECTION

INTERIOR TREE PIT A-A,
SCALE 1/2"=1'-0"

CROSS SECTION

8'X8' & 6'X6' TREE PLANTER TUBS B-B,
SCALE 1/2"=1'-0"

A-9

Appendix B
QUICK REFERENCE GUIDES

Plant Materials

The following lists of plant materials have specific growth characteristics that, under the proper conditions, have the capabilities to function as trees, shrubs, groundcovers, or vines in the interior landscape. Entries marked with an asterisk (*) can be found in chapter 4.

Trees

Araucaria bidwilli (Bunya Bunya)*

A. excelsa (Norfolk Island Pine)*

Brassaia actinophylla (Schefflera)*

Caryota mitis (Fishtail Palm)*

Chamaedorea costaricana (Costa Rican Palm)*

C. elegans (Parlor Palm)*

*C. seifrizii**

Chamaerops humilis (European Fan Palm)*

C. excelsa (Windmill Palm)

*Citrus arantiifolia**

*C. limonia**

*C. mitis**

*C. reticulata**

Crassula argentea (Jade Plant)*

Cycas circinalis (Fern Palm)*

C. revoluta (Sago Palm)*

Dizygotheca elegantissima (Thread-leaf Aralia)*

D. veitchii

*Dracaena deremensis**

D. draco (Dragon Tree)*

D. fragrans (Fragrant Dracaena)*

D. godseffiana (Gold Dust Dracaena)*

*D. goldieana**

D. indivisa (Dracaena Palm)

D. marginata (Dragon Tree)*

D. sanderiana (Ribbon Plant)*

Eucalyptus sp.

Ficus sp.*

Howea belmoreana (Curley Palm)*

H. forsterana (Paradise Palm)*

Lagerstroemia indica (Crape Myrtle)

Livistona chinensis (Chinese Fan Palm)*

Musa coccinea (Scarlet Banana)

Phoenix dactylifera (Date Palm)*

Podocarpus macrophyllus maki (Japanese Yew)*

Schefflera actinophylla (Umbrella Tree)

S. digitata (Seven Fingers)

Shrubs

*Abutilon darwinii**

A. calypha hispida (Copperleaf)*

A. wilkesiana (Painted Copperleaf)

Acfinidia chinensis (Chinese gooseberry)

Aechmea fasciata (Silver Vase)*

Agapanthus sp.*

Agave americana (Century Plant)*

Aglaonema sp.*

Allamanda sp.*

Amaryllis sp.*

Ananas comosus (Pineapple)*

Anthurium sp.*

Ardisia sp.*

Asparagus plumosus (Asparagus Fern)*

A. sprengeri (Sprengeri Fern)*

Aspidistra elatior (Cast Iron Plant)*

Aucuba japonica (Japanese Aucuba)*

A. j. variegata (Gold Dust Plant)*

Beaucarnea sp.*

Beloperone sp.*

Berberis thunbergii (Japanese Barberry)

Calceolaria sp.*

Callisia elegans (Striped Inch Plant)*

Camellia sp.*

Capsicum annuum (Red Pepper)*

Carissa grandiflora (Natal Palm)*

Chrysalidocarpus lutescens (Madagascar Palm)*

Chrysanthemum sp.*

Costus malortieanus (Stepladder Plant)*

*Cyperus alternifolius**

*C. papyrus**

Dieffenbachia sp.*

Gardenia jasminoides (Cape Jasmine)*

*G. radicans**

Kalanchoe sp.*

*Monstera deliciosa**

Pandanus veitchii (Screw Pine)*

Philodendron selloum (Split-leafed Philodendron)*

Pittosporum tobira (Japanese Pittosporum)

Polyscias balfouriana (Balfour Aralia)*

Ruellia sp.*

Spathiphyllum sp.*

Yucca aloifolia (Spanish Dagger)

Groundcovers and Vines

Achimenes sp.*

Acorus calamus (Sweet Flag)*

Adiantum capillus-veneris (Southern Maidenhair Fern)*

Adromischus maculatus (Calico Hearts)*

Aeschynanthus marmoratus (Zebra Basketvine)*

Aloe vera (True Aloe)*

Aphelandra chamissoniana (Zebra Plant)*

Asplenium nidus (Bird's Nest Fern)*

Begonia sp.*

Bertolonia sp.*

Billbergia sp.*

*Bougainvillea spectabilis**

Caladium sp.*

Calathea zebrina (Zebra Plant)*

Campanula sp.*

Ceropegia sandersonii (Parachute Plant)*

C. woodii (Chinese Lantern Plant)*

Chlorophytum comosum (Airplane Plant)*

Cissus rhombifolia (Grape Ivy)*

Coleus sp.*

Crocus sp.*

Episcia sp.*

Fatshedera lizei (Ivy Tree)*

Gynura aurantiaca (Purple Velvet Plant)*

Hedera sp. (Ivy)*

Hoya bella (Wax Plant)*

Maranta bicolor (Prayer Plant)*

Nephrolepis exaltata bostoniensis (Boston Fern)*

Peperomia sp.*

Pilea cadierei (Aluminum Plant)*

Sansevieria sp.*

Scindapsus sp.*

Sedum sp.*

Setcreasea purpurea (Purple Heart)*

Tradescantia fluminensis (Wandering Jew)*

Plants for Sunny Locations

This category usually indicates that the plants will receive at least five to six hours of direct sunlight during the winter months. Exposures to the east, southeast, or south are possible examples.

Abutilon
Acacia
Acalypha
Adromischus
Agapanthus
Agave
Allamanda
Aloe
Alternanthera
Amarcrinum
Amaryllis
Anacampseros
Ananas
Aporocactus
Astrophytum
Azalea
Bambusa
Bauhinia
Beaucarnea
Begonia
Beloperone
Billbergia
Bougainvillea
Bouvardia
Brunsvigia

Caladium
Calliandra
Callistemon
Calluna
Campanula
Capsicum
Carissa
Centaurea
Cephalocereus
Cereus
Cestrum
Chaenostoma
Chamaecereus
Chamaerops
Chorizema
Chrysanthemum
Citrus
Cobaea
Coccoloba
Codiaeum
Coleus
Conophytum
Cotyledon
Crassula
Crinum

Cuphea
Cyanotis
Cypella
Cyrtanthus
Cytisus
Dinteranthus
Dionaea
Echeveria
Echinocactus
Echinocereus
Echinopsis
Ensete
Erica
Eucalyptus
Eucomis
Eugenia
Euphorbia
Fatshedera
Faucaria
Feijoa
Felicia
Fenestraria
Fortunella
Fragaria
Freesia

Gazania
Gardenia
Gerbera
Gloriosa
Glottiphyllum
Graptopetalum
Grevillea
Gymnocalycium
Gynura
Habranthus
Haemanthus
Hebe
Hedera
Heliconia
Hibiscus
Hippeastrum
Hoodia
Hoya
Hydrangea
Hydrosme
Hylocereus
Impatiens
Ipomoea
Iresine
Ixora
Jasminum
Jatropha
Kalanchoe
Lachenalia
Lampranthus

Lantana
Lapeirousia
Leptospermum
Ligustrum
Lilium
Lithops
Lobivia
Lotus
Lycoris
Mahernia
Malpighia
Mammillaria
Mesembryanthemum
Mimulus
Moraea
Musa
Myrsine
Myrtus
Nerine
Nerium
Nicodemia
Nicotiana
Notocactus
Oliveranthus
Oplismenus
Opuntia
Oreopanax
Ornithogalum
Osmanthus
Oxalis

Pachyphytum
Pachyveria
Parthenocissus
Passiflora
Pelargonium
Pentas
Petunia
Phormium
Pittosporum
Pleiospilos
Plumbago
Polyscias
Portulacaria
Pseudosasa
Punica
Pyracantha
Rebutia
Rivina

Rochea
Rosa
Ruta
Sansevieria
Santolina
Sasa
Saxifraga
Schefflera
Scilla
Scutellaria
Sedum
Sempervivum
Senecio
Setcreasea
Solanum
Sprekelia
Stapelia
Stenotaphrum

Stephanotis
Strelitzia
Streptosolen
Synadenium
Tavaresia
Tetrapanax
Thevetia
Thunbergia
Titanopsis
Trifolium
Tulbaghia
Vallota
Veltheimia
Vitis
Zantedeschia
Zephyranthes

Plants for Semisunny Locations

This category usually indicates that the plants will receive two to five hours of direct sunlight during the winter months. North- or south-facing windows do not fit into this category.

Acanthus
Achimenes
Aechmea
Aeonium
Aerides
Aeschynanthus
Allophyton

Alloplectus
Alocasia
Alpinia
Angraecum
Aphelandra
Araucaria
Ardisia

Asarina
Ascocentrum
Asparagus
Begonia
Beloperone
Bletia
Boronia

Bowiea	*Cordyline*	*Fatshedera*	*Kaempferia*
Brassavola	*Costus*	*Fatsia*	*Koellikeria*
Browallia	*Crassula*	*Ficus*	*Kohleria*
Brunfelsia	*Crossandra*	*Fittonia*	*Lapageria*
Caladium	*Cryptanthus*	*Fragaria*	*Leea*
Calathea	*Ctenanthe*	*Fuchsia*	*Licuala*
Calceolaria	*Curcuma*	*Gardenia*	*Lycaste*
Callisia	*Cycas*	*Gasteria*	*Lygodium*
Camellia	*Cyclamen*	*Geogenanthus*	*Malpighia*
Carex	*Cymbalaria*	*Gesneria*	*Manettia*
Caryota	*Cymbidium*	*Gloxinia*	*Manihot*
Cattleya	*Cyperus*	*Guzmania*	*Maranta*
Ceropegia	*Dendrobium*	*Gynura*	*Mikania*
Chamaedorea	*Dichorisandra*	*Habenaria*	*Mimosa*
Chirita	*Dieffenbachia*	*Hatiora*	*Monstera*
Chlorophytum	*Dizygotheca*	*Haworthia*	*Muehlenbeckia*
Chrysalidocarpus	*Dracaena*	*Hedera*	*Musa*
Cibotium	*Dudleya*	*Hedychium*	*Nautilocalyx*
Cissus	*Dyckia*	*Heliconia*	*Neofinetia*
Clerodendrum	*Elaeagnus*	*Hippeastrum*	*Neomarica*
Clivia	*Ensete*	*Hoffmannia*	*Neoregelia*
Clusia	*Epidendrum*	*Homalomena*	*Nephrolepis*
Coccoloba	*Epiphyllum*	*Howeia*	*Nertera*
Codonanthe	*Episcia*	*Hoya*	*Nidularium*
Coffea	*Eranthemum*	*Huernia*	*Oncidium*
Coleus	*Eucharis*	*Hypocyrta*	*Ophiopogon*
Colocasia	*Euonymus*	*Hypoestes*	*Oplismenus*
Columnea	*Euphorbia*	*Impatiens*	*Pandanus*
Commelina	*Eurya*	*Ipomoea*	*Paphiopedilum*
Convallaria	*Exacum*	*Jacobinia*	*Parthenocissus*

Pedilanthus
Pellionia
Peperomia
Petrea
Phaius
Philodendron
Phoenix
Pilea
Piper
Pistia
Pitcairnia
Pittosporum
Platycerium
Plectranthus
Pleomele
Podocarpus
Polypodium
Primula
Pseuderanthemum
Pseudopanax
Reinhardtia
Rhapis
Rhipsalis
Rhoeo
Rhoicissus
Rivina
Ruellia
Saintpaulia
Sansevieria
Sarcococca

Sasa
Saxifraga
Schefflera
Schismatoglottis
Schizocentron
Schlumbergera
Scilla
Scindapsus
Scirpus
Selinicereus
Senecio
Serissa
Serjania
Siderasis

Sinningia
Smilax
Smithiantha
Sonerila
Sophronitis
Sparmannia
Spathicarpa
Spathiphyllum
Stenandrium
Streptocarpus
Strobilanthes
Syngonium
Tibouchina
Tillandsia

Tolmiea
Tradescantia
Vanda
Vanilla
Veltheimia
Vriesea
Wittrockia
Woodwardia
Zamia
Zantedeschia
Zebrina
Zygocactus

Plants for Semishady Locations

This category usually indicates that the plants will receive bright light, but no direct sunlight.

Achimenes
Acorus
Adiantum
Aechmea
Aglaonema
Amomum
Anthurium
Aspidistra
Asplenium
Athyrium
Aucuba

Begonia
Bertolonia
Blechnum
Brassavola
Caladium
Calathea
Ceropegia
Chamaedorea
Chamaeranthemum
Chlorophytum
Cissus

Cordyline
Cyperus
Cyrtomium
Darlingtonia
Davallia
Dieffenbachia
Dracaena
Episcia
Ficus
Fuchsia
Haemaria

Hedera
Helxine
Hemigraphis
Howeia
Lapageria
Lygodium
Maranta
Miltonia
Monstera
Nephrolepis
Nephthytis
Odontoglossum
Pandanus

Paphiopedilum
Pellaea
Pellionia
Peperomia
Phalaenopsis
Philodendron
Phoenix
Phyllitis
Physosiphon
Pilea
Pittosporum
Podocarpus
Polypodium

Polystichum
Pteris
Saintpaulia
Sansevieria
Schefflera
Scindapsus
Selaginella
Spathiphyllum
Syngonium
Woodwardia
Zamia

Plants for Shady Locations

This category usually indicates plants that tolerate low-light intensity but will not thrive in it.

Aglaonema
Amomum
Asparagus
Aspidistra
Chamaedorea
Chlorophytum
Cyperus
Dieffenbachia

Ficus
Hedera
Monstera
Nephrolepis
Nephthytis
Ophiopogon
Philodendron
Pittosporum

Podocarpus
Polypodium
Polystichum
Pteris
Sansevieria
Schefflera
Scindapsus
Syngonium

F-stop-to-footcandle Conversion Factor

$f/2 = 40$fc

$f/2.8 = 75$fc

$f/4 = 150$fc

$f/5.6 = 300$fc

$f/8 = 600$fc

$f/11 = 1,200$fc

$f/16 = 2,400$fc

Set the film-speed dial at ASA 25 and the shutter speed to 1/60th of a second. Place opaque white paper next to where the plants will be. Adjust the lens opening (*f*-stop) until the built-in meter indicates the correct exposure. (From *Interior Landcaping: A Study and Guide* by Robert Lindeblad, Department of Landscape Architecture, Kansas State University, 1975, pp. 16–17.)

Light-intensity Location Guide

Some planting areas are often designed before the structure itself is built or completed. To provide a data base for the selection of plant materials, the following represents the light intensities for *typical* locations.

Low Light Intensities (less than 75 fc)

- in front of a north-facing window obstructed by other plant materials (trees) or building overhangs.
- 4' to 6' (1.2 to 1.8 m) away from or 1' to 3' (.3 to .9 m) to either side of an unobstructed north window.
- at least 10' (3 m) back from or 2' to 4' (.6 to 1.2 m) to either side of an obstructed east or west window.

- 2' to 5' (.6 to 1.5 m) back from an obstructed east or west window.
- at least 10' (3 m) back from and 2' to 5' (.6 to 1.5 m) to either side of an obstructed south window.
- at least 15' (4.5 m) back from and 5' to 7' (1.5 to 2.1 m) to either side of an unobstructed south window.
- 6' to 8' (1.8 to 2.4 m) away from a 200 w incandescent reflector flood lamp.
- 10' to 12' (3 to 3.6 m) away from a 150 w incandescent reflector spot lamp.
- 7' to 9' (2.1 to 2.7 m) away from a 175 w color mercury vapor reflector lamp.

Medium Light Intensities (approximately 150 fc)

- directly in front of a north window, unobstructed
- directly in front of a partially (50%) obstructed east or west window.
- 3' to 5' (.7 to 1.5 m) away from 1' to 3' (.3 to .9 m) to either side of an unobstructed east or west window.
- directly in front of a fully obstructed south window.
- at least 10' (3 m) away from and 1' to 3' (.3 to .9 m) to either side of an unobstructed south window.
- 3' to 5' (.9 to 1.5 m) away from a 200 w incandescent reflector flood.
- 7' to 9' (2.1 to 2.7 m) away from a 150 w incandescent reflector spot.
- 3' to 5' (.9 to 1.5 m) away from a 175 w color corrected mercury vapor reflector flood.

High Light Intensities (approximately 300 fc)

- directly in front of an unobstructed east or west window.
- directly in front of a partially obstructed (50%) south window.
- 4' to 6' (1.2 to 1.8 m) away from or 1' to 3' (.3 to .9 m) to either side of a south window (unobstructed).
- 1' to 3' (.3 to .9 m) away from a 200 w incandescent reflector flood lamp.
- 3' to 5' (.9 to 1.5 m) away from a 150 w incandescent reflector flood.
- 2' to 4' (.6 to 1.2 m) away from a 175 w color corrected mercury vapor reflector flood lamp.

REFERENCES

Charbonneau, Gaston. *Tropical Plants*. Toronto, Ontario: Greey de Pencier Publications, 1975.

Doty, Walter L. *Sunset Western Garden Book*. Menlo Park, California: Lane Book Company, 1961.

Gaines, Richard L. *Interior Plantscaping*. New York: Architectural Record Books, 1977.

Herda, D.J. *Growing Trees Indoors*. Chicago: Nelson-Hall, 1979.

Hirsch, Doris F. *Indoor Plants*. Radnor, Pennsylvania: Chilton Book Company, 1977.

Lindeblad, Robert. *Interior Landscapes: A Study and Guide*. Manhattan, Kansas: Department of Landscape Architecture, Kansas State University, 1975.

Manaker, George H. *Interior Plantscapes*. Englewood Cliffs, New Jersey: Prentice-Hall, Inc., 1981.

McDonald, Elvin. *The World Book of House Plants*. New York: The World Publishing Company, 1963.

Scrivens, Stephen. *Interior Planting in Large Buildings*. London, England: The Architectural Press, 1980.

INDEX